Western Europe and the United States
The Uncertain Alliance

MICHAEL SMITH
Coventry (Lanchester) Polytechnic

University Association for Contemporary European Studies
George Allen & Unwin
London Boston Sydney

George Allen & Unwin (Publishers) Ltd,
40 Museum Street, London WC1A 1LU, UK

George Allen & Unwin (Publishers) Ltd,
Park Lane, Hemel Hempstead, Herts HP2 4TE, UK

Allen & Unwin, Inc.,
9 Winchester Terrace, Winchester, Mass. 01890, USA

George Allen & Unwin Australia Pty Ltd,
8 Napier Street, North Sydney, NSW 2060, Australia

First published in 1984

British Library Cataloguing in Publication Data

Smith, Michael, *1947 Apr. 10 –*
    Western Europe and the United States.—
(Studies on contemporary Europe; 6)
1. Europe—Foreign relations—United
States   2. United States—Foreign
relations—Europe
I. Title   II. Series
327'.094   D1065.U5
ISBN 0-04-327071-9
ISBN 0-04-327072-7 Pbk

Library of Congress Cataloging in Publication Data

Smith, Michael, 1947 –
    Western Europe and the United States.
(Studies on contemporary Europe; no. 6)
Bibliography: p.
Includes index.
1. Europe—Foreign relations—United States.
2. United States—Foreign relations—Europe.   3. Europe—
Foreign relations—1945–   . I. Title. II. Series:
Studies on contemporary Europe (European Association for
Contemporary European Studies); no. 6.
D1065.U5S65   1984   327.4'073   84–9252
ISBN 0-04-327071-9 (Allen & Unwin : alk. paper)
ISBN 0-04-327072-7 (Allen & Unwin : pbk. : alk. paper)

Set in 10 on 11 point Plantin by Grove Graphics, Tring, Hertfordshire
and printed in Great Britain
by Billing and Sons Ltd, London and Worcester

Contents

Editor's Preface

The University Association for Contemporary European Studies (UACES) exists to promote the study of contemporary European society in all its aspects. To do so it brings together a large number of scholars from many different disciplines. One motivating force for these scholars has been an awareness of the inadequacy of their particular scholarly discipline to provide satisfactory answers to the complex problems which they were handling both in research and in teaching. Many aspects of contemporary European economy, society and politics are indeed hard to illuminate if the light comes from only one of the traditional disciplines of academic study and this has meant that teachers, students and everybody else are frequently without adequate information on topics of immediate and important interest. The Association has therefore commissioned scholars currently working in such areas to present in short form studies of problems which are of special importance, or specially noteworthy because of the lack of easily accessible information about them in current public and academic discussion. The studies are written by experts in each particular topic. They are not, however, merely for teachers and students, but for anyone who may wish to find out something further about subjects which are now much discussed but about which real information is still hard to come by. In this way the Association hopes it may bring closer what are often the separate worlds of academic and public knowledge while at the same time providing a service to readers and students in a relatively new field of study.

ALAN S. MILWARD
*University of Manchester Institute
of Science and Technology*

Author's Preface

The author of any book digs deeply into the credit afforded by colleagues and friends. In this case, special thanks are due to Alan Milward, for his understanding and tolerance towards an errant author; to Dave Allen and Chris Farrands, for their helpful comments at various stages of the project; and to Evan Evans, the life-force of UACES, for simple encouragement. Joy Gardner and Jane Fox worked wonders in deciphering, typing and retyping the text and Stella Humphreys efficiently compiled the index. Any remaining errors, inaccuracies, or misjudgements are solely the responsibility of the author. Any inspiration the book contains is attributable to Dorothy, Kate and Caroline Smith, whose contribution in emotional and practical terms cannot be described in words alone.

MICHAEL SMITH
Coventry (Lanchester) Polytechnic

Introduction

Short studies of great subjects are at the same time both risky and essential enterprises. On one level, they flirt with the danger of oversimplification and superficiality, or with the tendency to stress the dramatic and the overtly 'important' at the expense of the subtle and complex relationships which may be penetrated only through more detailed and painstaking treatments. At another level, however, they can provide the interested but relatively uninitiated reader with the kind of panorama which will further stimulate interest, begin to give it a critical edge and provide a series of guideposts to further study. In setting out on this brief guide to relations between the United States and Western Europe in the period since the Second World War, I have been conscious of the importance and complexity of the subject (and thus of the risks of distortion), but also of the burning need for some kind of introductory treatment which could enable a fairly wide audience to achieve insight, understanding and persistence in their investigation of the European–American conundrum.

The Subject

There can be no doubt about the importance of the relationships which are generally subsumed within the umbrella term 'European–American relations'. In the sphere of diplomatic process, of negotiation and institution-building, the development since 1945 of a seemingly permanent set of links between a dominant United States and an initially weakened but later resurgent Western Europe has been the foundation of one of the most profound and continuous mutual involvements in modern international relations. This has been reinforced by the intimate strategic and security ties between the erstwhile great powers of Western Europe and the acknowledged superpower across the Atlantic – a relationship born in the Cold War, yet of equal and compelling importance in the era of détente and in the confusions of the 1980s. Finally, the diplomatic and the strategic entanglements of the United States and Western Europe have been accompanied by a growth of unparalleled economic interdependence, entailing mutual sensitivities and vulnerabilities of a degree experienced by no other group of nominally independent parties, and generating a large proportion of the world's international economic activity.

Thus, the European–American relationship is not only central to the affairs of the global system as a whole. It is also, on the sketchy evidence given above, a relationship of extreme complexity, in which activities at the governmental level coexist with and cut across those at the individual, commercial and international levels, and in which the seemingly neat and well-defined worlds of diplomacy, strategy and economic activity are inextricably interwoven. Not surprisingly, therefore, this intimate and multifaceted partnership has been a constant source and focus of debate, both at the level of academic analysis and at the level of political practice. In many cases European–American relations have been both the seed-bed and the test-bed for ideas, analyses and strategies which have become part and parcel of the broader international scene, and which have had ramifications far beyond the affairs of the North Atlantic area.

But what are 'European–American relations'? Already I have used the terms 'relations between the United States and Western Europe', 'North Atlantic area' and 'European–American relations', as well as other terms such as 'interdependence', 'partnership', 'institutions' and 'entanglements', all of which have different connotations depending on their context. The reader with any prior knowledge of this field will be well aware that no standard definition of the area exists, and that each author has a tendency to adopt the framework best suited to his or her immediate needs – yet another source of complexity and debate to which I will return at a later stage. At this stage, however, I should make clear the definition which I have adopted and which is central to the arguments put forward in the rest of this book. I shall use the terms 'European–American relations' and 'Euro-American system' to refer to the relations between the countries of Western Europe which are members of either the North Atlantic Treaty Organisation (NATO) or the European Economic Community (EEC),[1] or both, and the United States. Two characteristics of this definition should be emphasised. First, it excludes the countries of Scandinavia except those which belong to the groupings named, as well as the Eastern Mediterranean members of the EEC or NATO (Greece and Turkey) and the European neutrals, although reference will be made to these countries when necessary or helpful. Secondly, the definition is based on countries or societies, not simply on governments and their representatives – a matter of some importance in the light of the remarks I have already made about the range of connections which are a feature of European–American dealings. I have thus opted to stress the diversity of relationships between a slightly more restricted and central group of countries, rather than attempt to cover areas which have distinctive geographical, cultural, or other properties. Some basic data about the countries involved can be found in the table on p. 121.

The Approach

Despite the restrictions outlined above, the task of organising an introductory study remains daunting. I have thus decided on a second form of restriction, this one organisational and presentational rather than definitional. The approach of the book stresses the paradoxes inherent in the coexistence of continuity, change and uncertainty within European–American relations. It does so initially in three connected ways: by providing a framework of events; by examining the reactions of policy-makers; and by assessing the merits of academic interpretations (Part One). These themes are then developed in the central chapters of the book, which focus in turn on the settings within which European–American relations have developed or found expression, on the issues which have arisen between the countries involved in European–American relations and on the processes by which these issues have been pursued, managed, or fought out (Part Two). At the end of the book I return to the initial theme of uncertainties and debates, and attempt to cast some light on the possible future development of European–American relations in the light of the discussion overall. By adopting this method of organising my arguments and evidence, I hope that at least some of the complexity can be preserved, while the distinction between central and peripheral aspects of the relationships can be applied in a relatively clear-cut way. The following brief introduction to the arguments presented at various stages will help the reader to grasp the overall shape of the book.

Part One: an Uncertain Alliance

European–American relations in the period since the end of the Second World War have constantly troubled those who would for whatever purpose attempt to predict or regulate their course. As Alfred Grosser has pointed out in a recent and important study (Grosser, 1980), the origins of the relationship, and of the uncertainties which attended it from its very beginning, cannot precisely be located in 1945; indeed, many of the most significant trends and tensions were set in motion during the 1920s and 1930s. None the less, the beginning of a formal American 'presence' in and commitment to the affairs of Western Europe and the demand for a response on the part of West European governments and societies can legitimately be located in the later years of the Second World War. The relationship thus took shape in a period of uncertainty, a time at which fundamental changes in the structure of the international system were taking place, and was permeated by these surrounding uncertainties and changes. The uncertainties, however, did not stop there; indeed, it could be argued that the single most enduring characteristic of relations between the United States and Western Europe has been uncertainty – sometimes muted, sometimes thrown into stark relief, but never resolved or eliminated. As a consequence, the academics and political practitioners who have set out to crystallise, to cope with, or manage the central features of the relationship have arguably been doomed to frustration and anguish, until they have recognised the essential futility of their quest.

In Part One three elements or manifestations of this problem are identified and explored. First, there is a review of the period since 1945, paying particular attention to the tension between continuity, change and uncertainty (Chapter 1). Secondly, this is related to the doctrines and strategies adopted by policy-makers on both sides of the Atlantic, and to the tension between rhetoric and reality which has resulted (Chapter 2). Finally (also in Chapter 2), there is a review of some of the major academic approaches which have been used in the analysis of European–American relations, and of tensions between them. This initial review is designed to form the basis for further exploration of particular areas in succeeding chapters.

Part Two: the Architecture of Uncertainty

It becomes clear from the discussion in Chapters 1 and 2 that the links between Western Europe and the United States are inherently problematical, and that they are likely to defy efforts to achieve a comprehensive design or an exhaustive explanation. As already noted, however, this does not mean that they are an unrewarding subject for analysis; in fact, European–American relations are rich in the most far-reaching and instructive lessons for scholars and policy-makers alike. In Part Two of the study a framework for the analysis of European–American relations is developed, as a source of questions and an aid to critical inquiry. Like all other such frameworks, it cannot claim to be more than a device for organising and ordering inquiry; in this case, the underlying aim is also to establish more firmly the components of uncertainty and debate in the Euro-American system.

The framework advanced has three interrelated elements. First, it attempts to establish the variety and complexity of the *settings* within which European–American relations emerge and can be identified, on the assumption that the diversity and competing demands of these settings are related to the characteristic uncertainties of the relations in general (Chapter 3). Secondly, the framework sets out to isolate some of the major *issues* or sources of controversy and debate which have emerged in the course of relations between Western Europe and the United States since the end of the Second World War, on the assumption that the range and ramifications of these issues also contribute to the recurrence of uncertainty. Finally, the framework identifies some of the major *processes* by which European–American relations have been handled, on the assumption that the existence of a wide range of channels for action and interaction between the societies involved has emphasised the delicacy and unpredictability of policy-making and implementation.

It will be clear that these three elements cannot be separated in any terms or for any purposes other than those of analysis. In reality, the coexistence and mutual effects of the three are taken to be central to the persistence of the Euro-American system and of its besetting tensions. A systematic attempt at synthesis and reappraisal will be made in the concluding part of the book, although major areas of contact between the elements will be stressed at appropriate points in these three chapters.

As I noted earlier in this introduction, one of the central aims of this book is to stimulate and provide a framework for more detailed inquiry into European–American relations. As a consequence, the reader will find that much of the argument focuses on approaches and issues rather than a detailed description of events. I have also avoided the use of footnotes and detailed references in individual chapters, and have opted for a rather different form of reference to the literature. At the end of each chapter there is a brief guide to relevant references and sources, which is linked to an extensive annotated Bibliography. It is hoped that this will provide a fruitful compromise between the provision of a context for the argument and indications for useful further study.

Note: Introduction

1 I have adopted the term 'European Economic Community' throughout, although I recognise that in the 1980s the amalgamation of the three original Communities (the European Coal and Steel Community, ECSC; the European Atomic Energy Community, Euratom; and the European Economic Community) renders the term somewhat questionable. The major reason for my choice is simply that it would be confusing and counter-productive to chart all the changing usages; therefore, I have stuck with the central institutional focus and with its original title, which is still widely used as 'shorthand' for the whole range of European Community bodies. Where either the ECSC or Euratom is dealt with in its own right, it is naturally given its appropriate identity.

PART ONE

An Uncertain Alliance

1 Continuity and Change in European–American Relations

The study of European–American relations shares with many other branches of the social sciences a concern with continuity and change. It is clearly important for both academic analysis and practical diplomacy that the relatively stable and the relatively dynamic elements of world politics should be identified with as much clarity and certainty as possible, and that they should be evaluated in appropriate ways. Yet it is equally important for academics and practitioners alike to recognise that herein lies a central danger – that of coming to rely on assumptions and expectations which can be proved groundless by seemingly insignificant events or the unintended consequence of routine activities. In many ways the development of European–American relations since 1945 provides an object lesson in the dangers and difficulties of international change.

Between the ending of the Second World War and the outbreak of the Korean War in June 1950 there occurred a transformation in the links between the United States and Western Europe, the consequences of which are still much in evidence on both sides of the Atlantic. From a position in which there seemed a real danger that the United States might retreat to the prewar stance of isolationism, abjuring responsibility for the operation of a diplomatic system centred in Europe, there was created in a five-year period a framework of diplomatic, strategic and economic entanglement which has proved remarkably long-lived and adaptable. The impact of this change was felt at the time not only in terms of 'high diplomacy' and the larger pattern of international relations, but also in the domestic, political and social existence of Western European societies in particular.

This may appear unexceptional in the light of events since the later 1940s – the American 'presence' may be an uncomfortable fact of life for some West Europeans, but it is a fact of life none the less. In the late 1940s, though, the whole process of American entanglement was a focus of intense debate and controversy, and a good deal of uncertainty. For a start, it did not appear at the time to be at all inevitable that the

United States would become sucked into the affairs of Western Europe. Although the economic influence of American trade and finance had been felt throughout the 1920s and 1930s, the acceptance of practical responsibility for the affairs of Europe as a whole and Western Europe in particular was strictly limited by the strength of American isolationism. It is possible to see this kind of tension – between the needs of internationalism and the yearning for isolation – as a permanent motif of American international policy, but there is no doubt that in 1945 the balance between the two was very delicate indeed. The aims of American policy were consequently extremely difficult to identify. Were they focused on the promotion of a general 'concert' in which the United States, the Soviet Union and European countries would balance against each other, were they founded upon a 'grand design' for the world which would embody the American virtues of free trade and the 'open door' while continuing United States dominance in the military and economic fields, or were they aimed at the quickest possible retreat from the seamy affairs of the old world?

There was in fact a further alternative: that the United States government and its representatives had no clear policy or design, and that their entanglement in Europe resulted from an *ad hoc* series of responses to events which were later rationalised and codified by policymakers who felt the need to justify their positions. Such a judgement might be too extreme, but it seems clear that a range of global, regional and domestic pressures played a great part in moulding American involvement with Western Europe. Some of these pressures were of the kind which contributed to the Cold War in general – the perceived threat of expansion by the Soviet Union, which was especially pressing in the European arena. Others were more particular to Western Europe, where a series of factors combined to create a demand for American involvement and support. Among these West European factors, two in particular can be identified: first, the desire by a number of West European governments, and especially that of the United Kingdom, to get the Americans involved and keep them involved; and secondly, the fact that domestic political and economic weakness threatened to create a power vacuum in Western Europe which would endanger broader international stability.

These sets of factors, of course, could not be separated in reality as they have been here. Because there was a fluctuating and uneven balance between American priorities, Soviet pressures and Western European demands, the way in which American involvement developed was itself relatively unpredictable and untidy. Not only this, but the implications of American commitment were at best dimly discerned by those involved in the process. To be sure, by 1950 it was fairly clear in what areas commitments had been assumed. In the field of economic reconstruction and development the United States, through a mixture of trade measures, grants, loans and other forms of assistance generally subsumed under the umbrella of the Marshall Plan, had come to be an important provider of capital for West European industrial development. In their turn West Europeans, through the agency of the Organisation for European Economic Co-operation (OEEC), were committed to the exploration of avenues for greater co-operation. The field of military security, however, saw a rather less even balance. Through the North Atlantic Treaty, signed in April 1949 by the United States and eleven West European countries, the Americans had committed themselves to guarantee the security of countries in the North Atlantic area. This was essentially a one-sided commitment, because although the Treaty contained exhortations to 'self-help and mutual assistance', the plain fact was that of West European countries, only the United Kingdom could muster any significant independent defensive capability. American strategy recognised this, at least initially, by assuming that much of Western Europe might have to be conceded if the Soviet Union attacked, to be reconquered later. There was also a third area of American commitments – that of doctrine, primarily formalised through the Truman Doctrine enunciated in early 1947. By definition, such commitments as this – to assist governments threatened by anti-democratic forces – were bound to be unspecific and potentially all-encompassing in their implications, a danger borne out by the later fate of the doctrine of containment in Vietnam and elsewhere. In Western Europe itself the commitment to anti-communism led to active intervention by American diplomats and other groups in the domestic policies of Italy, and on a more limited scale in France, quite apart from the postwar involvement in occupied Germany.

By the 1950s, therefore, there already existed a complex set of mutual commitments involving the United States and Europe. There were distinct variations, however, both in the precision with which the commitments were set and in the degree of consensus between the United States and Western European countries about what the commitments meant. The greatest precision seemed to be in the Marshall Plan and its associated agencies, where the benefits provided were measurable and the West European contribution could be identified through the progress of the OEEC; but the closer one got to the areas of doctrine and military security, the less tangible became the bases of European–American collaboration, and the less consensus there appeared to be about the meaning of the mechanisms established. This was at least in part a reflection of uncertainties about the nature of the problems faced; how real *was* the Soviet threat, or the threat of communism in Western Europe? The Truman Doctrine and the American acceptance of the North Atlantic Treaty themselves reflected the impact of specific and threatening developments, which had a dynamic effect upon the perceptions of policy-makers in the United States especially, and the process was repeated with the onset of war in Korea during June 1950. Leaderships in Western Europe and the United States alike were quick to discern the possible analogy between a lightly defended South Korea and a Western Europe without the presence of substantial American forces.

The Korean War can thus be seen as ushering in a period of consolidation for the European–American relationship. It did not, however, signal an end to tensions and uncertainties about the way the relationship might be organised or conducted. Consolidation and elaboration were expressed most clearly in the strategic sphere, where the North Atlantic Treaty Organisation was established on a permanent basis with an integrated command structure. In the economic sphere the main initiative was a West European one, albeit with active American support: in 1950 the Schuman Plan put forward proposals for a European Coal and Steel Community which carried further the Marshall Plan's exhortations that West Europeans should enter into integration efforts. In the military and security field, however, progress was by no means as smooth, and this was nowhere more evident than in the controversy over German rearmament. American pressures for the rearmament of the newly established Federal Republic and for its incorporation into NATO aroused deep forebodings in France, whose government proposed the European Defence Community (EDC) as a more effective means of limiting West German military potential. As the Americans became more committed to the EDC idea during 1952 and 1953 it became clear that the French themselves might well be unable to secure its ratification; the result was mutual suspicion and recrimination. The situation was finally retrieved by an ingenious British compromise, by which the West Germans were associated with NATO through the device of Western European Union, and the EDC died a relatively quiet death.

German rearmament, however, was only part of a persistent uncertainty in the strategic and military field, largely caused by developments in the Cold War and Soviet–American relations. The Eisenhower administration which came to power in 1952 had to grapple with the problem of a growing Soviet military (and especially nuclear) capacity, at the same time as domestic demands pressed it to economise. The result was the 'New Look', a form of deterrence based on the threat of 'massive retaliation' by nuclear means against Soviet transgressions. In Western Europe the result was suspicion and uncertainty; the 'New Look' presented at one and the same time a demand that the countries of Western Europe should share more of the non-nuclear burden in NATO, and a threat that the massive use of nuclear weapons might be initiated without the formalities of consultation within the Alliance. At the same time, it was far from clear how far American support for and sympathy with the concerns of West European countries extended, given the Eisenhower government's view that the French and British colonial empires should be dismantled.

The result of these trends was an atmosphere of considerable tension, which was only increased by Soviet offers of concessions on Central Europe and the status of Germany during 1954–5. The tensions were compounded of domestic and international features, of economic burdens such as rearmament and questions of military doctrine, and of the frailties or miscalculations of leaderships in a number of countries. Hostility and recriminations reached a peak during 1954, with the EDC issue unresolved and the impact of French problems in Indochina at a critical stage; but by the middle of 1955 a lull appeared to have set in. The West Germans were in the process of being incorporated into the Western Alliance, economic reconstruction aided by the ECSC and the freeing of trade restrictions was well under way, and some of the doubts about the 'New Look' were laid to rest.

On the other hand, the very completion or consolidation of these trends carried with it a number of potentially important consequences. Although the elaboration of NATO had been carried forward, the developing United States–Soviet strategic balance continued to create ambivalences and conflicts of interest during the later 1950s, especially over two issues: the possession and control of nuclear weapons, and the status of Germany in general. The Soviet 'lead' in missile delivery systems, and the American attempts to extend their tactical nuclear presence in Europe, created major differences of view about the risks entailed in the developing nuclear balance. At the same time, proposals for disarmament and 'disengagement' in Central Europe, and the heightening of tensions over the status of Berlin, underlined disparities between American and West European perceptions. On the economic front the 'relaunching' of European integration which was to lead between 1955 and 1957 to the conclusion of the Treaty of Rome opened up new areas of uncertainty, relating to the extent of American support for a full-blown customs union such as that encapsulated in the European Economic Community (EEC); despite the inception of the Community in 1958, the unpredictability of events in this sphere was increased by persistent British support for a broader Atlantic free trade area, which was viewed with distaste by the sponsors of the EEC and with severe reservations by American policy-makers.

The period 1955–60 can therefore be seen as generating a ferment of new initiatives and trends, many of which were later to become causes of controversy and debate. Against this background, there also occurred a number of more limited incidents which had the effect of underlining European–American uncertainties. Perhaps the most dramatic of these was the Suez crisis (1956), which brought about a situation of open conflict within the Atlantic Alliance. The crisis itself only demonstrated in acute form some of the wider difficulties caused by change in the Middle East, where France and Britain retained substantial interests and bore the burden of colonial disputes. Meanwhile, the Soviet factor was not to be neglected: the growth of dissent within the Eastern bloc led to the suppression of the Hungarian uprising in 1956, and in the late

1950s the Berlin crisis refocused attention on the central arena of the Cold War. In the economic field the problems attending re-establishment of a convertible currency regime among the Western powers, and the transition from the OEEC to a new organising framework, the Organisation for Economic Co-operation and Development (OECD), brought home to many West European countries the hazards of an 'open' and flexible international economy. In domestic affairs the French especially experienced the impact of political instability, with the transition from the 4th to the 5th Republic and its attendant violence in France and Algeria.

By the beginning of the 1960s it was possible to take two opposed views of developments in European–American relations. On the one side, there was an impressive list of institutional and operational achievements, some of them on an explicitly Atlantic level and others within Western Europe, which lent substance to claims that a new kind of international community was emerging. On the other side, it was possible to point to numerous and persistent areas of contention – over strategic doctrines and responsibilities, over economic costs and benefits, and over the shape and legitimacy of West European political and social structures – which were highlighted by dramas such as those in the Middle East or the various theatres of Cold War. Nevertheless, to many it appeared that the 1960s heralded a new era of creativity and expansion: tensions within NATO did not in any way threaten the future of alliance, nor did they call into question the American commitment to Western Europe's security. In the same way, American political and business circles were conscious of a potential economic challenge from the new concentration of trading power in the EEC, but saw this as a small price to pay for the political benefits conferred by European integration and the new investment opportunities provided by a larger European market. On both sides of the Atlantic – but especially in the United States and West Germany – this was the dominant school of thought, far outweighing the reservations suppressed by those who emphasised the tensions and asymmetries in the embryonic 'Atlantic Community'.

It was in this spirit that the Kennedy administration, early in its life, began to develop the idea of an 'Atlantic partnership' – a political alignment which would go beyond the limits of conventional alliances and which would rely upon a relatively equal bargain between the United States and an expanded, integrating Western Europe. By the mid-1960s, however, this idea was far from being attained; indeed, the notion of 'Atlantic partnership', if it had ever been practical, had been undermined from a number of directions. In the first place, it appeared that the Americans were reluctant to consider any 'partnership' in which their dominance of the field of nuclear strategy might be eroded; in fact, the so-called 'McNamara Doctrine' enunciated in 1962, which centred on 'flexible response' to aggression, was based on centralised control of nuclear forces. This accorded ill with the policies of the French, especially – under de Gaulle, their fierce assertion of national independence created a transatlantic rift of major dimensions. Gaullism also fostered suspicion of the 'special relationship' between the United States and Britain, which was cited by the French leader as the central reason for his opposition to British entry into the EEC. The French veto, in January 1963, effectively thwarted any kind of 'united Europe' able to assume a role equal to that of the United States, and American policies in the next few years played a major part in sowing dissension between West European countries, whether by accident or design. Three areas of contention in particular can be mentioned here: the rather acrimonious negotiations over the trading relationship of the United States and the EEC, especially during the so-called Kennedy Round, allied with increasing suspicions in Western Europe of the challenge posed by large American corporations; the attempt to establish a Multilateral Nuclear Force (MLF) which especially affected the role of West Germany in relation to nuclear weapons; and the gradual American entanglement in Vietnam.

Far from constituting a 'partnership' or 'community', therefore, transatlantic relations by the end of the Johnson administration in 1968 seemed to form a battleground. The French withdrew from the NATO integrated command (though not the Treaty itself) in 1966; the MLF was shelved; trade and monetary relations were an area of further recriminations, especially in the light of a yawning deficit in the United States balance of payments. In addition, it appeared to many that the onset of Soviet–American détente after the 1962 Cuban missile crisis had redirected American attention; rather than a partnership with the awkward and diverse regimes of Western Europe, American policy-makers might be tempted to favour a 'condominium' organised by the superpowers. The aspirations of 1960 had become the contentious issues of 1967–8; or perhaps it was that the fundamentally uncertain and contested nature of European–American relations had reasserted itself, either through the actions of particular governments or leaders, or through the impact of underlying trends in the world economy and political system which would have strained the most intimate of communities.

When Lyndon Johnson announced his decision to 'retire' from the presidency in March 1968 European–American relations were thus once more in a condition of flux. Some of the reasons for this were of quite long standing – the Gaullist challenge, increasing American unease about their own position in the world economy, and the problems of 'burden-sharing' in NATO, for example. But the prospects for any 'normalisation' of relations were jeopardised by a number of more recent developments, which had undermined the confidence and self-images of societies and governments on both sides of the Atlantic. Already by 1968 it was clear that the trauma of Vietnam was having severe and unpredictable effects on American views both of their own world role and of the contribution expected from their allies. This trend was paralleled in Europe by the loss of confidence and stability which was to lead to the upheavals of 1968 in France and elsewhere. Meanwhile, the mid-1960s crisis had slowed the momentum and diminished the appeal of European economic integration at the same time as NATO was shaken by the French defection and American preoccupations elsewhere. The result was a transatlantic world in which the fragility of the regimes on both sides of the ocean was revealed, and in which 'Gaullism' or national self-assertion had its attractions for all concerned.

The scene was thus set for a turbulent period, one in which some of the illusions of the previous twenty years were to be shattered for better or for worse. In this process of change and fragmentation, the old order was challenged in both the strategic and the economic spheres; the challenge was sustained only with difficulty by the troubled regimes which experienced it. The strategic field was transformed partly because of a coincidence of interests between the United States and the Soviet Union, which grew out of the attainment of a 'stalemate' based on the rapid growth of Soviet nuclear capabilities. This was complemented by a change of attitudes and policy style in the United States especially, with the preference of Richard Nixon and Henry Kissinger for 'balance-of-power' policies and the pursuit of national interests rather than ideological crusades. Nixon and Kissinger developed the conception of a new 'structure of peace' in which major power centres would interact in a way reminiscent of the classical balance of power; in this structure the European allies were to play a full and responsible part. This reorientation of policy was encouraged by the Soviet Union, but it was clear that the part to be played by Western Europe was strictly limited. After all, American dominance in the field of nuclear weapons was undiluted, and this was what counted in the process of superpower détente. The result was a pervading and mutual suspicion: were the Americans and the Soviets doing deals at the expense of Western Europe? Would the Europeans play their part and bear the burden? Two episodes especially underlined the problem: the conclusion in 1968 of the Non-Proliferation Treaty (NPT) which applied in theory to all the allies; and the West German pursuit of *Ostpolitik*, which clashed at times with the global conceptions of the Americans by working for a relaxation of tensions in Central and Eastern Europe.

As the 'structure of peace' was elaborated the international economic order was collapsing. Although in 1967 the United States and the EEC played a major role in bringing the Kennedy Round of trade negotiations to a satisfactory conclusion, there had been evidence even then of differences of view. By 1968 it was clear that trade and other aspects of the Western order were threatened by a collapse of the monetary order established as recently as 1958. Economic divergences and the weakness of both the dollar and sterling placed immense pressure on the system of fixed exchange rates established under the Bretton Woods agreement; this was aggravated by French calls for a return to the gold standard and West German refusals to revalue their currency in line with their economic performance. The result was a series of massive speculative crises, fuelled by the very interdependence and mobility of capital which had been seen as the bases of a new Atlantic Community.

Between 1971 and 1973 the crisis reached a peak. In August 1971 the 'Nixon Shock' saw a devaluation of the dollar and a number of trade measures which signalled American rejection of the 'bankers" role in the Western economic system. By 1973 there was little left of the Bretton Woods system and the enlarged EEC was unable to muster any consistent position in the exchange rate chaos. Yet at the same time, the West Europeans were called upon to subscribe to the 'structure of peace' and (in April 1973) a 'new Atlantic Charter' which could form the basis of a new community. The so-called 'Year of Europe' proclaimed by Henry Kissinger ended in bitter recriminations, fuelled by the October War in the Middle East and the oil price crisis which followed. In 1974 there was to be an almost complete change of leadership in the major West European countries, as well as in the United States – but the new governments of Ford, Wilson, Schmidt and Giscard d'Estaing could hardly have relished the prospects for 'Atlantic Community'.

After the confusion and recriminations of the early 1970s, it might have been expected that there would be a 'breathing space' in relations between the United States and Western Europe; and indeed, during 1975 and 1976 there were frequent references to 'rebuilding', 'consolidation' and other worthy activities. The difficulty with these slogans was that although the crises of 1973 and 1974 appeared in some ways to be isolated and unexpected, the world had in fact changed; it had been undergoing transformations before 1973 and these continued after 1974. One aspect of the change might be described as 'globalisation': the process by which a lot of the problems in Euro-American relations came to have worldwide ramifications. Energy, trade, economic recession and industrial policy all had to be viewed in a system-wide rather than in a 'regional' or 'Atlantic' light, and the problems of management and co-ordination were correspondingly aggravated. This was not to say that specific 'Atlantic' problems disappeared – the 'chicken war' of the 1960s was followed in the 1970s by a 'cheese war', and in the 1980s by a 'steel war', while the problems of burden-sharing and consultation in NATO were still evident (see below). The point was, however, that 'Atlantic' problems could no longer be insulated from the disturbances which occurred in the outside world, even in the fevered imaginations of political leaders.

As indicated above, this was especially the case in relations between the United States and the EEC. The Kennedy Round of trade negotiations in the mid-1960s had found it hard enough to reduce tariffs and 'visible' barriers to trade in times of prosperity; the Tokyo Round, which began in the mid-1970s, had to deal both with such 'visible' protection and with 'invisible' discrimination applied through regulations or administrative devices at a time of recession and uncertainty. Within the EEC economic divergence between members exacerbated the problems caused by enlargement and made the aim of economic and monetary union seem an unattainable utopia. In 1978–9, however, some progress was made with the introduction of the European Monetary System (EMS) – largely as a defensive measure against American financial policy. The decline of the dollar, and American refusal to accept the responsibility of financial leadership, caused considerable disruption; no one, it appeared, was willing to bear the costs of policies needed to defeat inflation and recession. One result was to make industrial policy, and the management of surplus productive capacity, an international issue of the first order – steel, automobiles, shipbuilding and other areas became battlegrounds and revealed the problems caused by Japanese expansion for both the United States and Western Europe.

All of this indicated that the politicisation of economic activities had become almost complete, and that no longer was anything 'technical' or 'uncontroversial'. Least of all could this be said about the problems of energy and nuclear proliferation, which came to be linked under the Carter administration (1976–80). The Americans' failure to deal with the problem of their domestic oil consumption, and thus their need to import, caused recriminations with European countries, while their attempts to regulate the growing trade in nuclear technology led to yet more arguments and disputes. The ramifications spread in two main directions: first, into economic and financial co-operation, which seemed threatened by 'new nationalism' and protectionism; secondly, into the field of 'high politics', with the attempts of EEC countries to develop common foreign policy objectives through 'political co-operation'. In the Middle East this caused rumblings into 1983, while in other areas crises brought out the underlying differences of view (Iran, Poland and Afghanistan). It was not simply that European solidarity was questionable; American policies under Carter and Reagan exhibited confusion, internal competition and contradictions.

Many of the same symptoms were evident in the politics of NATO; indeed, the interpenetration of 'security' and 'economic' issues was both recognised by policy-makers and used by them. One area in which this process was (and is) visible was the familiar question of 'burden-sharing'. Despite a commitment in the late 1970s to increase their defence spending by 3 per cent per annum in real terms, all NATO members – including the United States – proved in varying degrees unable (or unwilling) to live up to their promises. The whole issue was entangled also with the problem of Theatre Nuclear Weapons (TNW) and Intermediate Range Nuclear Forces (INF) – an 'old chestnut' from the late 1950s, given added point by the Soviet deployment of new and more destructive missiles (especially the SS-20). American leaders, stressing the vulnerability of their existing forces, argued for massive increases in weaponry at the strategic and theatre levels. European leaders were caught in a major dilemma, wanting to ensure American commitment through acceptance of Cruise and Pershing II missiles, yet facing severe public opposition to any escalation of the nuclear arms race. Although the deployment of new weapons was explicitly presented as part of a 'two-track' policy, with an emphasis on the links between force modernisation and arms control negotiations, this did not resolve the problem. Only in 1982 and 1983 did it appear that American policy was beginning to respond, and to produce sustained attempts to allay the fears of Europeans by putting forward better-defined positions on the reduction of arsenals in both Western and Eastern Europe; but the potential Soviet response to such ideas as the 'zero option' in intermediate-range forces was far from clear itself.

It can be seen that there were major potential conflicts of interest here. These were made more damaging by the political fragility and uncertainties of regimes on both sides of the Atlantic, which caused misunderstandings and suspicions. For the Americans, the threat of 'Eurocommunism' in the mid-1970s was discerned especially in France and Italy (with noises-off from Spain and Portugal). Although this proved to be a 'paper tiger', the Washington leadership displayed persistent doubts about the reliability of some of its allies, which were compounded by disputes in the economic field and given new force by the nuclear controversies outlined above. At the same time, European leaders, in varying degrees, showed concern over the vacillations and riskiness of American policies in Latin America (El Salvador, Nicaragua and later Grenada), Asia (Iran and Afghanistan) and Europe itself (Poland). It was the last of these which brought many strands together: the interpretation of détente, the dangers of overcommitment in the new nuclear age, the price of economic sanctions, the acceptability of American attitudes (for instance, on human rights) in intimately involved Western European societies. By early 1983 doubts had been cast on the survival of the Western Alliance at a more fundamental level than ever before – but it was also clear that many of the doubts were the same as had attended its entire history, compounded by economic, military and social turmoil.

From this brief survey of the course of European–American relations since the end of the Second World War, two sets of conclusions can be drawn. The first set are empirical, relating to the substance of the relationship and to the changes which have occurred within it. It should be evident from what has been said that there are elements of considerable continuity in the development of European–American relations. In many areas, the issues, the institutions and the assumptions of the late 1940s are the issues, institutions and assumptions of the 1980s. But this very continuity of underlying concerns – with the solidarity of the Atlantic Alliance, the security of Western Europe, the prosperity and stability of industrial democracies – has meant that the manifestations and perceived significances of those concerns have been continually transformed by the impact of change in national societies, in the Atlantic area and the broader international system. We should thus not be surprised that the nature of the American commitment to Western Europe is an issue in 1983 as it was an issue in 1948; at the same time, we must allow for the fact that it is an issue in a radically different world, one in which attitudes, policies and institutions have undergone a process of continual transformation at national and international levels. Perhaps the major result of this coexistence of continuity and change has been recurrent uncertainty and a danger that events will outstrip the adaptive capacities of individuals, governments and societies alike.

This brings us to the second set of preliminary conclusions, which are important in a rather different way. Their orientation is analytical rather than empirical, in the sense that they deal with the interpretation of European–American relations at the policy-making and at the academic level. It is plausible to suppose that the dynamic elements and the uncertainty attending European–American relations have created – and will continue to create – special challenges for the policy-maker and the academic theorist, both of whom in different ways are dedicated to the task of systematising and predicting the course of what are naturally untidy sets of events and forces. The tensions and obstacles this has created for both sets of 'analysts' form the subject of Chapter 2.

Further Reading

There is no really comprehensive 'historical' treatment of European–American relations since 1945 – a fact which reflects the immensity of the subject. The closest approach is in Grosser (1980), an ambitious and interesting study which none the less favours the Franco-German dimension. DePorte (1979) gives a neat 'political' evaluation; Serfaty (1979) is useful on domestic impacts of American policy; Williams (1977) provides a compendious review of NATO and related topics. Schlesinger (1973) is an essential collection of documents for those wishing to study the 1945–73 period in depth. Anyone wishing to extend his or her awareness of events and debates eventually has to have recourse to the periodicals surveyed in the introduction to the Bibliography (pp. 122–24).

For specific periods or sets of developments, the range of treatments is extensive. A number of important studies and contributions are listed here for each decade (roughly).

1945–55: Secondary studies and collections include: Ball (1974); Beloff (1976); van der Beugel (1966); Diebold (1959); Etzold and Gaddis (1978); Fursdon (1980); Ireland (1981); Knorr (1959); Kolko and Kolko (1972); and McGeehan (1971). Some of the most notable memoirs also cover this period, in particular:

Acheson (1970); Adenauer (1966); Ball (1982); Eden (1960); Eisenhower (1963, 1966); Monnet (1978); and Truman (1965).

1955–65: Allowing for a little leeway in the late 1960s, the following are very useful: van der Beugel (1966); Brzezinski (1965); Camps (1967); Cromwell *et al.* (1969); Diebold (1960); Hoffmann (1968); Kissinger (1957, 1960, 1965); and Wilcox and Haviland (1963). Several of the memoirs already listed extend into this period.

1965–75: See especially the following: Camps (1972); Chace and Ravenal (1976); Cromwell (1978); Hanrieder (1974); Hoffmann (1978); Kaiser (1973, 1974); Landes (1977); Mally (1974); Osgood *et al.* (1973); Pfaltzgraff (1969); Rosecrance (1976); and Trezise (1975). The two volumes of memoirs by Kissinger (1979, 1982) also have much to say about the period.

1975–83: There are not so many major books on this period yet, but the following provide a range of views about the major continuing problems: Alting von Geusau (1983); Bergsten (1981); Bundy *et al.* (1982); Fedder (1980); Feld (1978); Freedman (1982); Hanrieder (1982); Hoffmann (1981); Joffe (1983); Kaiser and Schwartz (1977); Kolodziej (1980–1); Oye *et al.* (1979); Treverton (1980); and Tucker and Wrigley (1983).

2 Interpreting European–American Relations: Political and Academic Puzzles

Chapter 1 reviewed the course of events in European–American relations with the aim of identifying underlying processes of continuity and change. As noted at the end of that chapter, the coexistence and overlapping of problems and processes has created a major challenge for the 'systematisers' – both political and academic – who have tried to explain or theorise about the Atlantic scene. The argument in this chapter concerns this problem, and proceeds by examining in turn the difficulties facing the policy-maker and the academic theorist. The intention is to provide both a review of major schools of thought and a critique of some of their more obvious limitations in the light of the trends already surveyed.

Rhetoric and Reality in European–American Relations

All policy-makers face the problem of matching declaratory policy with operational policy – of producing deeds to match their words. In the international sphere, this problem is especially acute, since so few of the authority structures or shared assumptions which sustain domestic policy are present in developed form. One analyst of foreign policy has gone so far as to label it the 'purest of political acts', since it depends upon the exercise of political influence in its least institutionalised form. This being so, it is clear that declarations of intent, and statements of ideology or doctrine which in domestic politics might be translated into effective action, face the danger of frustration, and may indeed carry within them the seeds of their own destruction, when projected into the international arena.

European–American relations face this problem in a severe and often paradoxical form. On the one hand, it is clear from the arguments in Chapter 1 that this complex web of alignments, interdependencies and interests can render unpredictable the outcome of actions or policy initiatives taken in pursuit of ambitious or comprehensive designs. At the same time, the assumed affinities and shared concerns of the advanced industrial democracies which participate within the 'Euro-American system', can be seen as offering fertile ground for the development of common policies and collaborative action. Thus, European–American relations form a tempting stage for the declaration and hopeful pursuit of doctrines, while simultaneously ensuring that the policy-makers' quest is likely to be fruitless. An examination of the relationship between rhetoric and reality in relations between the United States and Western Europe bears out the force of this judgement.

It could be argued that the late 1940s and the 1950s offered the most favourable conditions for the balancing of declaratory and operational policy in European–American relations. The acknowledged imperatives of the Cold War and the Soviet threat, the weight of American pre-eminence, particularly in the military field, and the existence of close connections between elites and leadership groups on both sides of the Atlantic can be seen as a firm basis for the translation of doctrinal uniformity into practical collaboration. By the nature of the situation, the initiative in this sphere was taken by the United States and its policy-makers: these were the years of the Truman Doctrine, of 'containment' and the hawkish statements of John Foster Dulles on the subject of US/Soviet confrontation. Throughout the period, however, the sweeping declarations both of perceived threat and of hoped-for unity of purpose had to contend with the untidiness and nuances of West European politics. The interests and fears of West European societies and their governments were, it became apparent, diverse and often contradictory, and these same interests and fears were by no means necessarily those to which American policy-makers responded. Perversely, as it appeared to successive American administrations, the British felt that they could still play a major world role rather than acting as a member of the Atlantic Alliance alone. In the same way, the leaders of the 4th Republic in France obstinately adhered to a view of national needs and aspirations which was uncomfortable for Washington. Even the West Germans under Konrad Adenauer were given to pointing out the peculiarly sensitive position which they would occupy in the event of Dulles's more ambitious declarations coming to fruition.

The most spectacular demonstration of these divergencies was the crisis attending the German rearmament question and the European Defence Community between 1952 and 1954. There were other nagging failures by West European regimes to live up to their obligations – both doctrinal and material – within the Atlantic Alliance, but it was in the EDC controversy that the full ramifications of the great divide between rhetoric and reality emerged. From a position where the United States government in September 1951 was calling for West German rearmament and its incorporation in NATO, there was a retreat to reluctant acceptance of the EDC proposal, which promised to calm French fears and also to further the cause of European integration. While the Americans adopted the EDC as the symbol of Atlantic solidarity, they were met with British reservations and French inability to deliver on their declaratory commitments. In December 1953 Dulles delivered his notorious threat that there would be an 'agonizing reappraisal' of the American commitment in Western Europe if the EDC were rejected. Rejected it was, yet the disaster was prevented by precisely the kind of untidy compromise which American policy-makers were loath to envisage.

The same kind of contrast – between seemingly logical and desirable schemes for the amalgamation of European–American relations and the untidiness or recalcitrance of the real world – was demonstrated by the fate of President Kennedy's 'grand design' during the early and mid-1960s. First, unveiled by Kennedy during an Independence Day address in 1962, the 'grand design' was based on a 'declaration of interdependence' between the United States and a uniting Europe, which would form the basis of a burgeoning liberal world-system. As already noted, however, this interdependence and 'partnership' was conceived in radically different ways on the two sides of the Atlantic, particularly by the enthusiasts in Washington and the equally committed Gaullists in Paris. Where the Kennedy administration foresaw a military division of labour which left the United States with the whip-hand in nuclear weapons policy, the French in particular (but also the British) felt the need to emphasise their own nuclear capabilities. Where the Americans felt that the West European countries might play more of a role and bear more of the material burden in steering the world economy, the West Europeans were reluctant to dilute the benefits of the still embryonic EEC. Where the Kennedy administration called for a partnership in assisting the developing countries, the tendency in Western Europe was to stress the continuing need for European reconstruction.

This confrontation, sparked off at least in part by American attempts to set out a design for the development of European–American relations, came to be symbolised by the often bitter exchanges between Washington and Paris. De Gaulle's 'grand ambition' of a Europe reunited 'from the Atlantic to the Urals' on the basis of independent nations, by no means accorded to the aims of other major European actors, although the French government attempted to court West Germany in particular. The clash, whether expressed in terms of nuclear policy, of trade negotiations, or of diplomatic manoeuvre, provided further confirmation that the construction of 'grand designs' or blueprints for the management of European–American affairs was a hazardous enterprise.

In many ways, the decline and fall of the Johnson administration in the United States spelt the end of 'Atlantic partnership' as an aim of policy. Many, indeed, would argue that it ceased to be a major or immediate aim as soon as de Gaulle vetoed the entry of the United Kingdom into the EEC in January 1963. The waning of 'Atlanticism', however, did not put an end to the tensions between rhetoric and reality which seemed to have become part and parcel of European–American relations. During the 1960s one of the most consistent and effective critics of American policy had been Henry Kissinger, then a Harvard professor, who had argued that any notion of European–American 'partnership' had to be based on the devolution of real responsibility to a Western Europe whose interests would be found at some point to conflict with those of the United States. It was to be expected that when Kissinger achieved a central role in the formulation and conduct of American policy during the first presidency of Richard Nixon (1968–72), he would attempt to put into practice some of his earlier prescriptions. These expectations appeared to be on the way to fulfilment when the Nixon administration, promising a 'new realism' in foreign policy, set out to develop a 'structure of peace' based on a global balance of power, in which the 'new Europe' was to play a central role. To accompany this design, there was enunciated the so-called 'Nixon Doctrine', which stressed the responsibility of America's allies to carry the burden of their own defence in a constructive partnership with Washington.

The response in Western Europe to these designs and declarations should have been enthusiastic. With the departure of de Gaulle from the political scene in 1969, and with the renewed momentum of European integration which attended the anticipated entry of the United Kingdom, there seemed reason to suppose that a 'pentapolar world', a five-sided balance of power in which Western Europe could play a major part, was attainable. It was plain that if this were to be achieved, some progress towards political union in Western Europe was required, and that this should be accompanied by further moves in the economic and monetary field. As late as 1976 the Tindemans Report, on political union within Western Europe, identified these needs and also ringingly proclaimed that the first priority for a united Europe was to establish a working relationship with the United States.

Unfortunately, it had become clear in the early 1970s that such a 'working relationship' was likely to be very difficult to achieve. Once again, the reasons for the problems and failures seemed to proclaim the folly of setting out programmes for practical action in European–American relations. On the American side, the tendency of the Nixon regime to take unilateral action and to avoid tedious consultations with allies or associates found expression in the military field and on the economic front, with the progress of US/Soviet détente and the economic measures of 1971. In the case of Western Europe, the instability of the economic climate and the need to absorb new members into the EEC combined with the existing reluctance to bear greater burdens in NATO, in such a way as to reinforce the dependence of the European allies. A spectacular climax was reached with Henry Kissinger's ill-fated declaration of the 'Year of Europe' in April 1973; by the end of that year the idea of a responsible and wide-ranging collaboration between two approximately equal entities lay in ruins, as a result of events in the Middle East and the broader international field.

Perhaps understandably, during the late 1970s and the early 1980s the rhetoric of Atlanticism and 'partnership' was muted in European–American relations. The uncertainties of political leaderships both in Western Europe and the United States, and the impact of economic recession, forced policy-makers to a reluctant recognition that 'grand designs' were not appropriate to a complex and intractable world. On the other hand, the problem of matching declaratory policy with operational realities became evident at a number of sensitive points. President Carter began his term of office with what had become almost the ritual promise to consult with the European allies and to rebuild the shaky bridges across the Atlantic. At the same time, he proclaimed his determination to pursue human rights policies and to press for the full implementation of such agreements as the Helsinki Final Act of 1975 – a determination which caused predictable concern among European leaders living at rather closer quarters with the Soviet Union. By the end of his term of office Carter had changed direction to stress the strategic aspects of the United States confrontation with the Soviet Union, and the 'Carter Doctrine' sought to set limits to Soviet expansion in south-west Asia and the Middle East. Once again, the clash between the global declaration of American intent and the less sweeping ambitions of the West European allies was evident – more so in the Middle East because of the newly active role assumed there by EEC members through the mechanism of European Political Co-operation.

The election in 1980 of Ronald Reagan as President of the United States was accompanied by the promise to mend fences and refurbish the Atlantic partnership. Again, however, it became clear that declarations of faith and good intentions were still difficult to translate into effective policy. Increasing tension in the military and strategic fields led to predictions of a 'new Cold War', but the simple verities of the Cold War could not be re-established in the changed world of the 1980s. West European governments were castigated by Americans as 'partial partners', wanting to shelter under the American nuclear umbrella while trading with the enemy; the United States government proclaimed its determination to stamp out high-technology transfer to the Soviet Union but was in turn attacked by the West Europeans for not applying sanctions to its own grain and other exports. The rhetoric of European Political Co-operation, especially on Middle East affairs, irritated Americans who could not see the EEC devoting resources or 'muscle' to the cause, while European leaders feared the consequences of renewed American crusades against unfriendly forces. By the beginning of 1983 it appeared that despite the continued affirmations of Atlantic understanding and solidarity, European–American relations were in a state of chaos and confusion.

It should be clear from the discussion here that this dichotomy – between stated affinities and actual disparities of interests and policies – has been a constant feature of European–American relations since the late 1940s. Such a preliminary conclusion suggests that the problems lie not in individual actions, leaders, or policies, but in the nature of the relationships themselves. In later chapters this proposition will be examined at greater length, but at this point it must be left as an intriguing avenue for exploration, and one which further emphasises the uncertainties of Atlantic relations. Having looked at the ways in which those uncertainties might influence the schemes and expectations of policy-makers, it is now necessary to examine their relationship to the academic interpretation of European–American relations.

Analysis and Explanation in European Relations

In somewhat the same way that the designs of policy-makers have continually been confounded by the untidy realities and complexities of European–American relations, so have the designs of academic analysts. The academic study of international relations has long been an arena for contention between divergent perspectives, none of which in the end furnishes a complete or satisfactory explanation of the global system. To this general trend, the policy of European–American relations has been no exception; indeed, many of the more contentious debates have had at least part of their origins in the political processes of the North Atlantic area. Given the wide range and the complexity of relations between the societies involved in the Euro-American system, it would be foolish to suggest that any one academic perspective could fully describe the 'nature of the beast' or explain its workings. There is an additional complicating factor here, in the fact that many 'academic' analyses of European–American relations have been produced in close proximity to the policy-making community, and that they have often (as in the case of Kissinger's writings) been designed to alter the view of policy-makers themselves, especially in the United States. One of the more important elements in a critical approach to the study of this area is thus a keen awareness of the extent to which there is an interaction between the academic research agenda and the preoccupations of policy-makers.

In the light of what has just been said, it is hardly surprising that one of the longest-established and most powerful approaches to European–American relations is what might be called the 'politics of power and security'. This approach generally rests upon three interrelated assumptions: first, that the international system is a state system, and that to all intents and purposes the actors within the system can be reduced to states and their representatives; secondly, that the major concern of states is the maintenance of their security in a hostile and competitive world; and finally, that security is best assured by a combination of policies aimed at the achievement of a favourable power position, either through purely national measures or through collaborative mechanisms such as alliances. Besides being for a long time the dominant perspective in the study of international relations more generally, it is often claimed that such a set of assumptions forms the basis of actions and interpretations by policy-making 'practitioners'.

Viewed in this way, European–American relations become comprehensible as an expression of interstate relations and the ceaseless quest for security. After the Second World War the efforts of policy-makers on both sides of the Atlantic were bent towards the re-establishment and the stabilisation of a state system in the chaos of Europe – both American policy and the efforts made by governments in Western Europe had the effect of restoring and of returning legitimacy to an international structure which was different in form but not in essence from that which had characterised the prewar world. The greatest stimulus to this process, and the element which paradoxically assured its continuing utility, was the existence of an immediate and urgent threat posed by the Soviet Union and its perceived expansionism. In the face of this threat, the search for security was of the highest importance, and security was assured by the construction of a remarkable alliance system centred on NATO. Despite recurrent differences of opinion, and occasional overt challenges within this structure, the whole edifice, it is argued, has been remarkably stable and in a sense 'successful'. Analytically, therefore, the Euro-American system represents a case study in the persistence of traditional concerns within the interstate system, and especially in the ways in which alliances and the balance of power can be used to cope with the demands of international security.

Within this seemingly neat and reassuring framework, however, there have been constant debates and controversies between academic analysts, which have often reflected the course of events in the real world of European–American diplomacy. The Euro-American system might be a state system, but it is and has been possessed of a singular structure, in which power is concentrated largely in the hands of one member. Among the other members, there have been attempts to promote new structures which appear to transcend the state system as it is conventionally understood (especially the EEC). Periodically, there have been great doubts about the legitimacy or the status of certain members, caused by their inability or unwillingness to 'play by the rules' of the system. What is the academic analyst to make of these apparent mutations in what appears to be a state system of a familiar kind? There have not only been uncertainties about the components and structure of the system, but also nagging doubts about the functioning of the mechanism, especially in the central area of security. For a state system based on collaboration in the face of an external threat, the Euro-American system has displayed alarming fluctuations and divergencies in its members' perceptions of their security problems. From time to time members have acted as if the threat did not exist, and have taken to fraternising with the enemy; at other times they have insisted that the threat must be met on a far broader front than that provided by the Atlantic Alliance, and that both domestic intervention and foreign adventures are legitimate responses. Governments have been known to act as if the threat and the Alliance could be ignored, and as if the pursuit of economic advantage could safely be accorded precedence over the dictates of security or the balance of power. Faced by these seeming contradictions, the 'power and security' analyst, or the 'political realist', can take refuge in either or both of two related positions: first, that there has been a constantly shifting balance of power and of national perceptions since the initial consolidation of the Euro-American system; and secondly, that there has been no real change in the underlying reality of power relations. The problem is thus still essentially the same, but its form and its implications have exhibited constant change.

While this might be good enough for some analysts, others have mounted sustained and far-reaching attacks on the well-defended positions of 'power and security'. Not only has the form taken by the problem changed since the late 1940s but, they would claim, the problem itself is a different one from that conceived by the 'political realist'. One of the most pervasive schools of thought is that which contrasts the assumptions of a traditional 'power and security' view with the new idea of 'complex interdependence'. According to this line of argument, world politics can only make sense if a number of traditional assumptions are either relaxed or discarded. First, it can no longer be assumed that states are the sole or even the dominant actors on the world stage; the reality is a system of mixed actors, in which states have to coexist with organised groups ranging from humanitarian lobbies to multinational businesses, which pursue a multitude of purposes, and which sometimes play by different 'rules' from those associated with the state system. Secondly, and as a result of the expansion of the range of actors within the system, there has emerged a multiplicity of channels and processes for the conduct of international 'business'. Some of these demands may be provided by governments and their representatives; many are not, and can operate beyond the immediate control of governments. Thirdly, the assumed predominance of security issues on the international 'agenda' has been undermined by the growth of issues related to economic and social welfare, and by the emergence of new areas of political concern for governments and other groups alike. Finally, much of what is done in the international arena is no longer done through the use of traditional mechanisms such as force or high-level diplomacy; the changing context has dictated an emphasis on complex processes of bargaining, the building of coalitions and the use of indirect influence.

Seen from this perspective, European–American relations take on a new complexion. No longer do they appear as the product of actions and policies emanating solely from states and governments, Instead, they represent the combined interests and activities of a range of groups including governments, commercial enterprises, private interest groups, and international and transnational institutions. Almost everything which occurs, and almost everybody who acts within and between the societies of Western Europe and the United States, is potentially relevant to the Euro-American system. There is none the less a system, which is built upon the burgeoning numbers of transactions which take place between those societies and which is held together by the fact that withdrawal from it would be costly in economic and political terms for all concerned. The history of European–American relations since 1945 thus has to be rewritten, in terms of the growing mutual involvements of the societies concerned – the expansion of trade, of business travel, of tourism and of financial interpenetration. At the root of this process is a recognition by governments and other groups that their purposes can no longer be achieved by action at a purely national level. Governments can no longer ensure the security or the welfare of their citizens without resorting to extranational methods, while a vast range of other groups and individuals find they can profit from the freedom of manoeuvre afforded by the 'open societies' of Western Europe and the United States. Threats to security and the reassertion of national independence are thus less immediate problems than the maximisation of welfare and the easing of international transactions. Strategies are conceived in terms of technical refinements and in terms of their implications for domestic and governmental subgroups, rather than in terms of national action and 'high diplomacy'. There is thus not one alliance, or one balance of power; there is a multitude of shifting alignments and coalitions aimed at furthering the interests of specialised and often surprising constituencies.

Clearly, one of the great virtues of an analysis based on 'complex interdependence' rather than on the traditional 'power and security' assumptions is that it helps to account for a number of otherwise puzzling and disturbing aspects of European–American relations. The state system may not work as predicted because it is not the only system; security issues may not always be at the top of the international agenda because the agenda fluctuates and is subject to many extraneous influences; the politics of alliance and the balance of power are not the only tests of international order or harmony. As with the position of the 'political realist', the assumptions are reassuring: after all, the Euro-American system appears to be held together by myriad bonds of mutual advantage, and to possess a resilience which is founded upon a genuine fund of common interests. Unfortunately, there are also areas of uncertainty and obscurity which tend to complicate the analysis. Perhaps the most important of these relates to the position of national states and governments, which have perversely refused to accept that their autonomy and their control over events have been eroded within the Euro-American system. Although some analysts of the growth of interdependence explicitly argue that national states have lost control of their foreign relations, and that this applies especially to the 'modernised' states of the Atlantic area, there has been a good deal of evidence during the 1970s and 1980s that the state's resilience has been underestimated. Not only does it appear that some states are able to re-erect barriers against the tide of interdependence; it is also evident that interdependence can be used as a weapon with which to exploit the vulnerabilities of other societies, by linking together issues and forcing the pace of negotiations or management processes. It also seems that the salience of 'interdependence' as a replacement for the 'old' politics of 'power and security' is related at least in some degree to the climate of action in Soviet–American relations, and that the heightening of tensions during the early 1980s has enabled some more traditional 'agenda items' to re-establish themselves.

In a sense, the debate between exponents of 'power and security' or 'interdependence' views of European-American relations is one which can be transferred to the overall study of international relations. This can less easily be said of a third analytical approach to the area, which focuses on integration and community-building. This is not to say that such a focus is unique to the study of the North Atlantic area or the Euro-American system; it is undeniable, however, that it has found its fullest and most elaborate expression there. Ideas of international integration and international community can be seen as building upon and going beyond the analyses of both 'power and security' and 'interdependence'; they take the existence of shared concerns and interests and of high levels of interaction as their raw material, and proceed to argue that particular sets of relations are so intensive or intimate as to transcend the normal constraints of international dealings. In this perspective, the major actors are elites and interest groups possessing close mutual contacts and a high degree of mutual responsiveness. It is their patterns of communication and shared experience which form the building-blocks of an integrated community in both the political and the economic spheres. The eventual (assumed) result of this process is the establishment of some kind of international social system which transcends the limitations of the national state and becomes the repository of loyalties and values which would otherwise find expression in nationalistic and mutually destructive competition. It can be seen from this brief description that such a perspective is not merely descriptive or explanatory; it possesses a strong and explicit value element based on the assumption that international community is a 'good thing'.

As already noted, the major expression of such a view has been in terms of the relationship between the United States and Western Europe. Shared forms of economic and political structures, cultural affinities and interpenetrations and a uniquely high level of mutual transactions have been seen by a number of analysts as making the Euro-American system a test-bed for ideas of political integration and community. In its crudest form, the assumption has been that there has been and will be a growth of common interests and policies which will virtually produce a single political and economic unit; in more sophisticated expressions, it is assumed that a degree of pluralism will always remain but that there will be significant differences between European–American relations and 'ordinary' international dealings. The high point in the production of such ideas occurred in the early and mid-1960s, at a time when the notion of 'Atlantic partnership' was high on the agenda for policy-makers, especially in the United States. At the same time, the progress of European economic integration seemed likely to consolidate one of the major building-blocks of a broader community.

It can be seen that the perspective of integration and community-building has been closely related to events in the real world and to the preferences or preoccupations of policy-makers. The same might be said of the two perspectives examined earlier – 'power and security' and 'interdependence' – but the base for integration and community-building has been more restricted and fragile than for either of these views. As the 1960s progressed, and both European integration and 'Atlantic partnership' entered turbulent waters, it became clear that there were central areas of uncertainty in the analysis of integration and community. First, it became apparent that regional economic integration could not be relied upon as a cumulative process destined to provide the major building-block of a broader unity in Western Europe, and academic analysis became far more inclined to deal with the EEC as a special case of 'normal' international relations than to see it as the precursor of a new world. Secondly, the idea of 'Atlantic partnership' came to be interpreted by some less as a foundation for a true community than as a vehicle for the exercise of American dominance – a form of acceptable hegemony, disguising the reality of American ideological and political mastery. The troubles encountered by both the European and the Atlantic versions of community-building were emphasised for many analysts by the emergence of parochial and neo-nationalist tendencies in both the economic and the broader political fields during the 1970s and early 1980s.

The antidote to many of the more optimistic prognostications for the growth of either a European or an Atlantic community is contained in a final perspective on European–American relations, which focuses on the contradictions and struggle inherent in the relationship. Some of the elements in this perspective are of long standing, building as it does on Marxist and radical ideas of the conflicts between classes and concentrations of capital in the world economy, but they were given added force in the 1960s and 1970s by the emergence of European–American clashes and the aggravating effects of general recession. In this perspective, the major actors (if that is an appropriate word to use) are classes, particularly the owners of capital, who may and often will enlist the support of the state as a channel for the pursuit of their class objectives. These objectives are expressed in terms of domination and systematic exploitation of other groups, through the perpetuation of a structure which consolidates the power and privileges of the capitalist class. The outcome of this process is a situation of perpetual struggle, at times muted, which eventually bears within it the seeds of destruction for the dominant class. At the international level certain consequences follow: the development of some areas of the world at the expense of others, and the growth of contradictions between rich capitalist countries which can lead to open conflict.

All of this is a far cry from the assumption that international interdependence and the growth of community are a dominant feature of European–American relations. A very different image of the Euro-American system results, in which the determining force is the relationship between West European and American capital, and the shifting balance of advantage between them. In the immediate postwar period the dominance of American capital expressed particularly through the Marshall Plan and the establishment of a 'liberal' world monetary and trading system enabled the United States to deal with Western Europe as part of its sphere of influence. The foundation and development of the EEC was designed to bolster this sphere of influence, but had the paradoxical effect of creating a dynamic and growing concentration of West European capital, which came to be engaged in a struggle with American capitalism. This struggle has taken many forms: the attempt to restrain the influence of large American firms and to create 'European firms' in retaliation; the extension of the EEC's 'sphere of influence' to a number of Third World countries which are tied by mechanisms such as trade and aid agreements; the heightened international competition in many industries created by the onset of recession and the scramble for markets for surplus production. According to some analysts – Marxist and non-Marxist alike – the eventual consequence might be a collapse of the post Second World War influence structure, with consequences as radical as an alignment between Western Europe and the Soviet Union in a transformed international system.

No one could call this a cosy view of the way in which European–American relations have developed in the past or might develop in the future. It posits with great certainty the occurrence of the kinds of conflict which have been muted in the period since the Second World War, and points to the temporary nature of the alignments which many, both in the United States and in Western Europe, accept as immutable. This is not to say, however, that this perspective does not have its limitations and 'blind spots', as do the others which have been examined here. Most important, the emphasis on contradictions and struggle seems to downgrade the evident resilience of the Euro-American alignment, and of the forces which are committed to its maintenance. As has been noted, these are both powerful and persistent, although subject to their own frailties and limitations; they range through the shared experiences and perceptions of the 'Atlanticist' elite to the broader power-political elements of challenge and response associated with the Cold War and strategic bipolarity, and to the perceived mutual benefits of continuing and enhanced economic interdependence. The net result is a store of creativity and mutual responsiveness which might not ultimately prevent the heightening of contradictions between the societies of Western Europe and the United States, but which at the very least could postpone it for a considerable time. Consequently, radical and Marxist analysts have had periodically to reconsider some of the conclusions they have drawn about the certainty of a fundamental change in the international structure, although this may not invalidate the overall force of their arguments.

For the student or concerned observer of European–American relations, the result of this analytical diversity and of the tensions between different schools of thought can be bewilderment or disillusionment. The Euro-American system can seem to be such an indeterminate or contested concept that it is hardly worth pursuing. In reality, the reverse of this is true: European–American relations form a battleground between scholars, as they do between the designs of policy-makers, but the result of the contest is far from negative. None of the schools of thought here surveyed can provide an exhaustive description or interpretation of the links between societies in Western Europe and the United States, but each of them furnishes useful questions and evidence about the functioning and development of this 'uncertain alliance'. Each of them has its orientation towards the three dimensions explored in the second part of this book – the settings, issues and processes associated with the Euro-American system – and each will be explicitly reassessed in the final part of the study.

Further Reading

The problems explored in this chapter are often dealt with, either explicitly or implicitly, by the general reviews of European–American relations. Thus, for example, Grosser (1980) deals at considerable length with the clashes of doctrine between American and European leaderships. Serfaty (1979) also has a good deal to say about policy-makers' attempts to discern or reinforce elements of 'design' in transatlantic relations. DePorte (1979) is a self-conscious attempt to interpret relations between the European states and the superpowers in terms of the development and consolidation of a 'state system'. In addition, a useful review of several of the perspectives examined in the second half of the chapter can be found in Smith *et al.* (1981): see especially the selections by Bull, Hanrieder, Morse and Rothstein.

In relation to the two major areas of inquiry in the chapter, the following are a representative sample of treatments.

Rhetoric and reality: For the period 1945–55, see Kissinger (1957, 1960); Kolko and Kolko (1972); and van der Beugel (1966). On the 'grand design' and 'Atlantic partnership', see: Cromwell *et al.* (1969); Hoffmann (1968); Kissinger (1965); Kleiman (1964); Kraft (1962); Munk (1964); and Wilcox and Haviland (1963). The Nixon–Kissinger period is very well covered by, for example: Cromwell (1978); Kaiser (1974); Kissinger (1979, 1982); Mally (1974); *Orbis* (1973); Osgood *et al.* (1973); and Schaetzel (1975). Finally, the late 1970s and early 1980s can be sampled from: Hoffmann (1978); Kolodziej (1980–1); Pfaltzgraff (1975); and Tucker (1981). This list covers a wide variety of types of sources, and a wide variety of viewpoints, but gives an indication of the richness of the material.

Analysis and explanation: The 'power and security' or 'realist' approach is in fact very well represented among the views of policy-makers dealt with above. DePorte (1979) as already noted takes such a view. See also: Fedder (1973, 1980); Hoffmann (1968, 1978); Kolodziej (1980–1); and Treverton (1980). Approaches centred on 'interdependence' can be sampled in Camps (1974); Cooper (1968); Czempiel and Rustow (1976); Feld (1978); Keohane and Nye (1977); Oye *et al.* (1979); and Wallace (1976). The 'integration and community-building' perspective, as noted, has periodically attracted much attention. Among the more revealing treatments are: Cleveland (1966); Deutsch *et al.* (1969); Goodman (1975); Hahn and Pfaltzgraff (1979); Kaiser (1966–7); Kaiser and Schwartz (1977); Pfaltzgraff (1969); and Richardson (1964–5). The structural conflicts and contradictions built into transatlantic relations are explored (from a variety of points of view) in: Calleo (1965, 1970, 1982); Calleo and Rowland (1973); Kaldor (1979); Mandel (1970); Servan-Schreiber (1968); Wallerstein (1980); and Whitman (1975). Two studies which stress the general intractability and diversity of the Euro-American system, in different ways, are: Chace and Ravenal (1976); and Smith (1978). It should be remembered, of course, that the divisions between schools of thought and perspectives are highlighted here; there is often much overlap between the views of writers who adopt differing overall approaches.

PART TWO

The Architecture of Uncertainty

3 Settings: The Environment of European–American Relations

Many theories of social action, whether in the domestic or the international field, rely upon the notion that the demands imposed and opportunities presented by the environment are a major limiting factor, both on the way in which action is taken and on the ways in which it might take effect. Without going so far as to adopt a theory of environmental determinism, it can be argued that the setting of social action plays a major part in shaping the action's success, failure, or practicality. If European–American relations are conceived in this light, as a product of actions emanating from the societies of Western Europe and the United States, then it is important to be aware that there are a variety of settings which might facilitate, limit, or confound the actions involved, and thus contribute to the occurrence of uncertainties and tensions. In this chapter four such settings of European–American relations are examined: first, the global arena; secondly, the Atlantic system; thirdly, Western Europe itself; and finally, the domestic arenas of the societies concerned.

The Global Arena

In many ways the expansion and formalisation of European–American relations in the late 1940s and early 1950s reflected a global process – the ending of the Second World War, and the delineation of the 'lines of battle' for the Cold War confrontation between the United States and the Soviet Union. Europe as a whole, rather than Western Europe *per se*, was the cockpit of the early Cold War tensions, arising from the disputes over the postwar status of Germany, Poland and other defeated countries. For the purposes of this analysis it is most important to bear in mind that Europe – and the division of Europe which enabled use of the term 'Western Europe' itself – was central to the evolution of Soviet–American confrontation. In Western Europe also the concentration of American attention and resources during the early Cold War years created the most elaborate and institutionalised of the Cold

War alliances, through the mechanisms of NATO and the parallel economic activities of the Marshall Plan. It is equally important, however, to remember that even in its earliest stages the Cold War was not simply European (let alone West European) in its ramifications and impact. The major stimulus to the transformation of NATO into a permanent, integrated military machine was provided by the Korean War, and the attention of the American leadership was frequently turned elsewhere, to Indochina or to East Asia.

During the 1950s and 1960s the importance of the Cold War's extra-European dimensions became evident. Two major aspects of this process are central to the setting of European–American relations: first, the globalisation of Cold War activities; and secondly, the growing obsession of Americans and other policy-makers with the global strategic balance between the United States and Soviet Union. The first trend meant that American policy-makers in particular faced demands on their attention and resources from an ever-widening set of clients and a proliferating series of conflicts – a stimulus to the kind of overextension which later brought humiliating reverses in Vietnam and elsewhere. The second trend – towards an almost exclusive concern with the strategic balance between Washington and Moscow – again placed demands upon the American policy machine which were bound to have an impact on relations with Western Europe. Cold War confrontation in Western and Central Europe, in so far as it involved the active participation of West European governments, was primarily based on the prevention of a conventional attack by Soviet forces and on the easing of tensions in other fields; the development of a global nuclear stalemate thus threatened to separate the West European and the broader issues.

Tensions of a similar kind could be identified as the Cold War became transformed into détente during the later 1960s. Just as the broadening of the Cold War confrontation had changed the significance and perceived value of European–American relations, so the onset of détente posed challenges and opportunities in the operation of the Euro-American system. In the first place, détente promised to have a great impact on Western Europe and on the character of relations between West European societies and the Eastern bloc. It was not quite so clear, however, what role the West Europeans were to play, or what were the limits of the détente process. Many of the threats, challenges and opportunities which were features of the late 1960s and early 1970s were of central importance to West European societies and governments – the 1968 crisis in Czechoslovakia, the Strategic Arms Limitation Talks (SALT) and the opening up of commercial contacts between East and West – but it appeared that the Americans either through choice or compulsion were led to deal with them at a global level. The same interpretation could be placed upon the growing American/Soviet tensions of the late 1970s and early 1980s: American policies on human rights, on trade with the Soviet Union and on military strategy were fraught with implications for the West Europeans, especially when tested by crises such as those in Iran, Afghanistan, or Poland. However, West European demands and interests often clashed with the global imperatives which impressed themselves on policy-makers in Washington, and demonstrated a certain ambivalence about Western Europe's proper role within the global arena. Disputes over sanctions against the Soviet Union and Poland particularly led to recriminations in 1981 and 1982, with American leaders accusing the Europeans of a narrow 'regionalism'.

This expressed a contrast between assumptions of American 'globalism' and West European 'regionalism' which has been a constant theme in the evolution of European–American relations. From a situation in the 1920s and 1930s which was almost exactly the opposite – the Europeans involved in and obsessed by the operation of the global system, the Americans introspective and inactive – there was a crossover in the early years of the Cold War. Although the British and the French cherished aspirations of a continuing global role during the 1950s, their abilities to fulfil it were limited to say the least; the Americans, reluctantly at first but with growing zeal, took up the burden. This led to a series of what might be called 'transition crises', with the French (in Indochina and Algeria) and the British (in the Mediterranean and the Middle East) confronting both the limitations of their own power and the growing ascendency of the United States. The most spectacular such crisis occurred over Suez in 1956: a dramatic manifestation of a continuing trend, and a humiliation which left its mark in subsequent British and French policies. In such circumstances, a 'regional' obsession with economic reconstruction seemed more appropriate to European needs.

If anything, during the 1960s the trend was reinforced and given added momentum, but neither West European governments nor those in Washington found it easy to cope with the new roles and expectations which resulted. A major reinforcing factor was the growth and elaboration of regional integration in Western Europe, but it remained uncertain what the end-point of the integration process might be. Was 'Europe' to become a kind of superstate capable of sustaining a role in the international system akin to and alongside that of the superpowers, or was it to remain a 'civil power', with areas of unity and influence in the economic and technical fields but little in the way of an integrated and global 'foreign policy' of the traditional kind? At the same time, the optimism of the Kennedy years in the United States – when the willingness to 'go anywhere and pay any price' in defence of Western interests was a source of self-confidence and of the impetus to widespread interventions – was difficult for American leaders to sustain. In the changing global arena there appeared to be more enemies or doubters than friends, and friends were often found to be demanding clients.

These two areas of ambiguity – West European reluctance or inability to act as a 'proper' support for American policies in the global field, and the latter's interventionism which gave rise to fears of escalation and overextension – were central to the way in which European–American relations responded to the demands of the broader international system at this time.

As already noted, the contrast between American globalism and West European regionalism was underlined at many points during the evolution of Soviet–American détente. Indeed, it came to be part of the Nixon–Kissinger foreign policy doctrine that in default of its ability to play a full part in the 'pentapolar world', Western Europe had to be assigned a purely regional role, with regional interests. Only the United States seemed capable of mustering the authority to act as a global manager, and this assumption was reflected in Kissinger's call for a 'New Atlantic Charter' during the 'Year of Europe' (1973). For a year or two thereafter, the mobility and the authority of American diplomacy, personified by Kissinger himself, formed a stark contrast with the regional and economic obsessions of Western European governments. During the late 1970s, however, the contrast became blurred, with important consequences for the roles of the United States and Western Europe in the global arena. First, there emerged a new and more positive tone to attempts at foreign policy collaboration in Western Europe, particularly through the European Communities but also in the context of such processes as the Western economic summits. It appeared as a result that West European governments might have more to say on a broad range of global problems, by no means all of them purely 'economic'. Simultaneously, there emerged doubts about the capacity or willingness of American administrations to sustain a global management role or to dominate events as much as they had during the 1960s. There was an uneasy balance in American policy between the desires for a 'new isolationism' and for a new moral crusade – a dilemma which found its fullest expression in the policies of the Carter administration between 1976 and 1980.

As a result, a subtle and far-reaching shift in the links between European–American relations and the broader global arena could be identified – a shift which continued into the 1980s and which was accentuated by both the political and economic crises of the new decade. Afghanistan, Iran, Poland and the Middle East all tested the new 'rules of the game' and (as we shall see later) often found them sadly underdeveloped. Along with these developments in the political and diplomatic field, however, went others which were arguably even more far-reaching in their implications. World politics, to put it crudely, was spreading, to encompass areas which had previously not been politicised and to invade new domains where the 'rules of the game' and the hierarchy were by no means indisputable. Thus, new fields of contention were almost bound to emerge, calling for creative responses both from West European countries and from American administrations: among the most remarked of these new domains were those of North–South relations, energy and industrial policy. As will be seen in Chapters 4 and 5, the working out of the consequent disputes did not supplant the old 'agenda' of European–American issues, but instead greatly expanded and supplemented it.

The Atlantic System

It is clear from the discussion so far that no analysis of European–American relations can divorce them from the broader global arena, which has provided both a series of demands and opportunities and an arena for action. Many of the most important elements in the setting of European–American relations, however, have a more explicitly and specifically 'Atlantic' origin, reflecting the structure of relations and the mutual pressures operating between societies in the North Atlantic area. While the global arena provides much of the scenery against which European–American relations have developed, the Atlantic system is responsible for many of the more tangible and immediate aspects of the relationship.

In the late 1940s the most tangible and immediate feature of the Atlantic system was the emergence of a structured set of mutual obligations and commitments between the West European countries and the United States. The North Atlantic Treaty, signed in April 1949, committed the signatories to aid each other in case of aggression within a defined geographical area (later expanded), and also to enter into 'continuous and effective self-help and mutual assistance'. Thus, it provided both an immediate guarantee and the opportunity of further institutionalisation and development. Neither the nature of the guarantee nor the provision for future development was entirely clear, however: it thus became apparent in the early years of the Alliance and with the growth of a permanent organisation that the expectations and interests of the countries involved were often divergent. During the early 1950s the tensions between fears of a Soviet attack and the danger of German rearmament revealed some of the ambiguities in the framework; the Suez episode in 1956 uncovered differences of view about the extent to which Alliance partners should retain their solidarity outside the area of the formal commitment; and the problems of the 1960s and the 1970s with military regimes in Greece and Turkey further revealed the contestability of the assumptions behind the formal structure of NATO.

One aspect of the Atlantic strategic system which did seem incontestable was the overwhelming predominance of the United States in terms of capability – of men, money and military hardware. For many

Europeans, the problem this created was a simple one – how to get as much of this capability as possible committed as irrevocably as possible to the defence of Western Europe. In the early years of the Alliance the efforts of governments in Britain, West Germany and France alike were bent towards the maximisation of American contributions to NATO and to ensuring that the United States would live up to its obligations. Nowhere was this more marked than in the field of nuclear strategy; after all, it was one of the most compelling features of the Atlantic strategic balance that only the Americans had a major nuclear capability. This area of American predominance has been one of the fundamental environmental factors in the course of European–American relations from the 1940s to the 1980s. Like all environmental factors, however, it can be (and has been) interpreted in a variety of ways. From the start, American administrations accepted the obligation to provide a nuclear defence for Western Europe; on the other hand, they persistently tried to get West European countries to bear more of the burden on the conventional warfare front, and occasionally hinted that the nuclear obligation could be met without involving American forces in Western Europe itself. Governments in Western Europe, in contrast, generally accepted the United States commitment in the nuclear field (although sometimes fearing it might be either over- or underenthusiastic), but held a rather different view of their own obligations in the conventional field. This issue will be taken up at greater length in Chapter 4, but here it serves to indicate the extent to which the range and measure of American predominance in the strategic field has been a vital aspect of the Atlantic system.

In terms of formal obligations and institutions, and of the balance of capabilities, it might be argued that relatively little has changed in the Atlantic strategic setting over the past thirty-five years. To be sure, the British and French have developed small nuclear forces; equally, the French, the Greeks and the Turks have at various times and for various reasons been alienated from the Alliance, while the Spanish have gradually worked their way towards it, but otherwise it might easily be seen as a constant in European–American relations. To anyone familiar with the events of the 1970s and 1980s, however, this is a difficult argument to sustain. In fact, at times during these years there appeared to be a very real danger of the Alliance becoming unglued and of the inherent contradictions in commitments and capabilities reaching breaking-point.

There appear to have been three major reasons for this phenomenon, some of them connected to the global factors dealt with in the preceding section. First, the impact of détente on the Alliance was problematical: after all, NATO is not obviously well-equipped to act as a vehicle of reform and reconciliation, and the focus of détente on the political shape of Central Europe called into question the relevance of many of the organisation's underlying assumptions. At the same time, a second set of forces were working to shake the NATO structure. For many members of the Alliance, it was no longer clear that it formed an appropriate focus for their interests. For some, this reflected a projection of interests into the global arena rather than Europe itself; while for others, it reflected a disinclination to bear the burdens and the risks of alliance in a changing world. Associated with this was a third and more specific factor: the decline of American dominance in its broader sense, which unleashed a number of corrosive forces. If the Americans were becoming an 'ordinary country' in the economic and political fields, might they not feel inclined to become more 'ordinary' in the military and strategic field, thus eroding their commitment to NATO? Whether or not this were to happen, the decline in American assertiveness and willingness to bear the burden of leadership, which became more pronounced as the 1970s progressed, had damaging effects, partly because of its patchy and unpredictable impact.

It is thus debatable whether the seemingly impressive and well-founded structure of the Alliance has formed a constant element in the setting of European–American relations. Commitments have wavered, been eroded, or undergone amendment; capabilities have been a matter of debate and contention; and purposes and priorities have been contested and obscured. Part of the reason of this set of ailments can be found in a second component of the Atlantic setting, the growth and functioning of the Atlantic economy. Throughout the history of the 'Western Alliance', it has been assumed that the strategic affinities manifested in NATO are paralleled by affinities of economic organisation and interests. Indeed, as already noted, the economic structures of Atlantic relations began to take shape through the Marshall Plan and the OEEC, even before the creation of an Alliance structure. In the minds of many policy-makers during the late 1940s and early 1950s, there was a close connection between the security provided by the North Atlantic Treaty and NATO and that provided by economic recovery in Western Europe. As a result, an economic regime emerged at the Atlantic level, embodying a range of material undertakings as well as a series of more or less explicit aspirations. The material undertakings were focused particularly on the achievement of a rapid economic recovery in Western Europe, primed by the provision of American aid through grants and loans. The aspirations were less capable of immediate realisation, but at least in the eyes of American policy-makers they were equally important: they involved the completion of a liberal trading system based on non-discrimination, a system of fully convertible currencies and a major relaxation of international controls over the mobility of capital. Each of these aspirations in turn had to yield to the imperatives of West European reconstruction, and each of them was far less cherished by policy-makers in battered European economies than by their American adherents.

Gradually during the 1950s some of the aspirations for a liberal Atlantic economic system were realised. Equally evident, however, was the basic contradiction between some of the economic structures and practices emerging in Western Europe and the framework of liberal 'Atlanticism' – a contradiction which forms the backdrop to many of the contentious issues surveyed in Chapter 4. While the General Agreement on Tariffs and Trade (GATT) and the Organisation for Economic Co-operation and Development (OECD, the expanded successor to the OEEC) were confirmed as the watchdogs of a liberal trading structure, the EEC emerged in the late 1950s as a trading bloc with significant protectionist features such as the Common External Tariff and (by the early 1960s) the Common Agricultural Policy. While the convertibility of major West European currencies was established in 1958, the frailty of some economies gave governments a continuing incentive to control financial transactions and flows of capital. At the same time, the upsurge of investment in Western Europe by American corporations during the early and mid-1960s had two important effects: it aroused fears in Western Europe that this could be a form of 'invasion by stealth', undermining national control of economies, and it aggravated an existing American balance-of-payments problem largely created by military expenditure in West European countries.

The contestable nature of much of the Atlantic economic structure was mitigated to a certain extent by the economic dominance of the United States. In much the same way as the Americans could underwrite the security needs of Western Europe, it appeared that they could underwrite its economic needs, from their extensive financial and commercial resources. Thus, the dollar formed a medium of exchange as good as gold, and could be used to pay the bills of an Atlantic trading system; American trade could stand the strain of continuing protectionism in Western Europe, in the cause of reconstruction and economic security; and the funds of American multinationals could form an invaluable injection into West European economies starved of high technology and capital investment. When the Suez Canal was closed in 1956, the Americans could even resupply the West Europeans with oil from their own domestic production to make good the shortfall from Arab sources.

By the early 1960s, however, this position was beginning to change, and in changing it revealed starkly the irreconcilability of the West Europeans' needs and the Americans' aspirations. The most significant aspect of the change was the emergence of a substantial and continuing deficit in the American balance of payments, which led to consequent pressures upon the dollar and upon the whole regime of fixed currency parities and free convertibility. This was not a deficit on the current account of visible trade; rather, it was created by massive transfers of capital from the United States to Western Europe, among other areas of the world. It was aggravated by a slowing of domestic economic growth in the United States, by an acceleration of inflation there and, finally, by the disruptive consequences of the war in Vietnam. At the same time, the economies of EEC members in particular were booming, producing substantial and sustained growth in production and employment.

In effect, during the mid- and late 1960s the landscape of Atlantic economic relations was transformed. This is not to say that the economies of West European societies suddenly established a kind of parity with that of the United States; indeed, during the late 1960s there was much concern in Western Europe over the so-called 'technology gap', which was seen as reflecting American superiority in high-technology research and development, and over the challenge posed by American multinational corporations. This took second place, however, to the problems caused by the collapse of the monetary and financial regime hitherto sustained by the dollar. The real climax of this process came in 1971, with the economic measures taken by the Nixon regime. These included a devaluation of the dollar, and various discriminatory trade measures, with the implied aim of making the United States an 'ordinary country' in international financial and commercial dealings.

The problem was that it was effectively impossible, even during the later 1970s, for the economic influence of the United States in the Atlantic system to be 'ordinary' – and this contradiction of American policy formed an essential part of the developing Atlantic setting. Whether or not American policy-makers saw themselves as pursuing national interests or some broader economic philosophy, the American economy was still a dominant factor in the Western economic structure, not least because of the dollar's role in financing world trade. To be sure, there appeared to be challengers – the European Community and Japan – but in a sense their challenges were one-dimensional, focused on relatively limited economic sectors and without the backing of political design and authority. Willy Brandt, in a famous phrase, once termed West Germany 'an economic giant but a political dwarf'. Increasingly, this contrast seemed to apply to the role of Western European societies within the Atlantic economy as a whole, and to make for a substantial disparity between the economic balance and the political/strategic balance in the Atlantic system.

The responses of American and West European leaderships alike were uncertain: on the American side, a continuing pressure for the Europeans to bear more of the economic burden, and take some of the responsibility for lifting the world out of recession; on the European side, a feeling that the American administration, whether under Carter or Reagan, failed to recognise the residual power of their economic muscle and the responsibility they still bore to organise the Western economic system. The specific areas of contention, which symptomised this set of underlying tensions, will be surveyed in Chapter 4, but in the present context the shifting balance of economic influence and leadership within the Atlantic economy is the crucial element to be emphasised. By the early 1980s a position had been reached in which, for a combination of domestic and broader international reasons, the effort of organising a collective 'Atlantic' response to the ailments afflicting the international economy seemed to be beyond the capacities of the Atlantic nations.

When this set of economic tensions was combined with the political and strategic tensions already surveyed, it appeared that a secular decline in the salience or impact of the Atlantic setting might form a major element in relations between the United States and Western Europe. It also appeared that this decline was associated with the erosion of a third part of the Atlantic system, the kind of 'community of values' which had been thought to sustain it in good times and bad. In the early postwar years it had seemed relevant to point to the kinds of cultural and ideological affinities which characterised European–American relations and to see them as building-blocks for a broader kind of community. The interpenetration of European and American cultures, with the United States appearing as precursor of the new world and a land of opportunity while Western Europe appeared as the fount of much that passed into the cultural, philosophical and academic life of the United States, was a source of this aspiration. There were, however, more material bases for these affinities and the enhanced responsiveness to which they were said to give rise. During the early years of the Cold War there was a premium on the elevation of ideological and institutional convergence between the United States and Western European societies, a kind of ideological and institutional alliance to match the alliances which emerged in the strategic and economic fields. Not only this, but there was a very powerful bond at the elite level between those who had run the wartime effort and who occupied important peacetime roles on both sides of the Atlantic. Perhaps the most famous of such elite groupings was that which surrounded Jean Monnet, the instigator of many of the most crucial initiatives in the European integration process, and which included both American and European leaders.

It would thus appear that the postwar 'Atlantic community' was sustained not only by economic and strategic realities but also by the less tangible ties of elite responsiveness and ideological convergence. Through the early years of NATO and the EEC, despite the buffets caused by crises within and outside Europe, there was a broad consensus upon the limits of acceptable behaviour and on the kinds of values to be pursued within the Western Alliance. Just as the economic and strategic structures of the Atlantic system threatened to come unglued in the 1960s and 1970s, however, so did the transatlantic value consensus. The reasons for this were in many ways the same as those in the economic and strategic spheres – a recovery of self-confidence and a reassertion of diversity in Western Europe, the decline of American leadership and confidence, and the loosening of ideological ties in the global system more generally. Thus, the self-assertiveness of Gaullist France, of Chancellor Brandt's Germany and of communist parties in a number of West European societies can be seen as reflecting the crumbling of Atlantic values; in the same way, the shifting foundations of presidential power in the United States, away from the East Coast to the south or the west, have been seen as injecting a new perspective into the handling of Atlantic affairs. Above all, the simple passing of time and the dying-out of the postwar 'Atlanticist' elite has washed away the accumulated store of shared experiences and shared values which enabled Jean Monnet to be *persona grata* in the highest councils of governments on both sides of the European–American divide and has reduced the ranks of the opinion-makers who could convince populations of the rightness of the Atlantic emphasis. The mutual European–American recriminations of the early 1980s might thus be seen as a symptom of divergent expectations and experiences, in ways which those of the 1950s and 1960s were not.

By the 1980s, therefore, it was apparent that the setting of European–American relations was radically different from that of the 1940s, not only at the global but also at the transatlantic level. It would be wrong to pretend that the Atlantic system of the early postwar years functioned smoothly and on the basis of complete mutual understanding, just as it would be wrong to argue that in the 1980s the system had become completely unstable. The truth for both periods – and those in between – lies somewhere in the middle, with a mixture of community and contention as the dominant features of the setting, complicating the calculations and actions of all those involved.

European–American Relations in Western Europe

In discussions of the global scene or of the Atlantic system, it can easily be forgotten that Western Europe itself is not an entity comparable to a state or even a superpower (a lapse of memory which has afflicted American policy-makers on more than one occasion). However one conceives of Western Europe – as a congeries of independent states, as a potentially united superstate, or as something in between – it is apparent that in itself it provides a setting for European–American relations. The United States has played a central and enduring role in the emergence of economic integration in Western Europe, and has established a major presence in West European societies. It is important, therefore, to be aware of the symptoms and implications of European–American relations within the setting of Western Europe itself, and to relate those to the broader settings already examined in this chapter.

An inescapable feature of relations between the United States and the societies of Western Europe in the aftermath of the Second World War was that in a very real sense the Americans had 'invaded' Western Europe. To be sure, this invasion was sought after and regarded as essential by the liberated areas, although there was a clear difference between the kind of American presence established in Britain, France and the Benelux countries and that imposed on West Germany and Italy. It would not be going too far to say that the American presence – sometimes only reluctantly countenanced by politicians in the United States – was a determining feature in the shaping of postwar West European society, moulding the political and economic forces of the reconstructed continent. Sometimes this moulding influence was openly and positively exercised, as in the establishment of the Federal Republic of Germany (West Germany) in 1949, although how much of this process reflected conscious planning and how much the pressure of events has been a cause of much scholarly debate. In other cases American intervention was less all-embracing, although still significant – for example, in the working out of postwar political arrangements for Italy, especially in ruling out communist participation within the newly established regime. In yet other situations the mere presence within West European societies of large numbers of alien personnel, reflecting the economic and social expectations of a different continent, was a continued matter for concern. The terms of the American presence were in many ways formalised between 1949 and 1952, through the establishment of NATO, the working out of the earliest stages of European economic integration and the consolidation of postwar rule by non-communist political forces. This did not, however, render the presence uninfluential or uncontroversial, and three fields of interest in particular can be identified for the whole postwar period: the military, the economic and the social.

In the military field, the consolidation of NATO as a permanent organisation with an integrated command provided the framework for a quasi-permanent American military presence in Western Europe. In particular countries this overall framework was supplemented by agreements for the provision and use of military bases and other facilities (in the case of Spain, not a member of NATO until 1982, the base agreements had much the same effect as in other NATO member-countries). During the 1950s the presence was consolidated through agreements on the numbers of American forces to be committed to NATO, and through the building up of an elaborate military establishment involving both nuclear and conventional forces. The establishment of such a permanent and sophisticated presence contained a number of paradoxes, however, bringing both benefits and penalties for the societies in which it was implanted. For some societies the paradoxes were those which came of being defended at the possible cost of nuclear destruction; in West Germany especially the mid-1950s brought the realisation that they would be the first victims of a nuclear exchange. In other cases, as with the French, the contradiction centred upon the loss of sovereignty entailed in being defended by an alien presence, without the luxury of full consultation or guaranteed influence.

On the other side of the coin, there were tensions in the American position on a permanent military commitment to Western Europe, which became more apparent as the 1960s unfolded and the problems of the American economy multiplied. Maintaining a major physical presence in societies which at times appeared less than grateful for the protection thus afforded, at substantial cost which was not met fully by 'offset payments', and in circumstances where the host societies appeared unwilling to bear their full share of the NATO defensive burden, came to appear as an imposition on American goodwill. By the late 1960s disputes over the framework of the American presence had reached a level at which plans substantially to cut the American commitment were seriously contemplated. Although these were never fully implemented, the paradox of the American military presence has never disappeared; in the late 1970s it reappeared in sharpened form with the plans to station new forces of Cruise missiles and Pershing IIs, which were initially sought by West European governments and later became the subject of grave doubts at the popular and elite levels. As the doubts grew so did congressional pressures in the United States to limit or reduce the American presence.

Similar internal contradictions have always attended the American economic presence in Western Europe. Given the ways in which the Allied effort had been organised during wartime, it was inevitable that the role of the American forces and administrators in postwar Europe would have an economic dimension. In occupied Germany this was seen at its clearest, with the occupation forces responsible for organising industrial production and carrying out the economic provisions of the Potsdam Agreements; but in other arenas the American presence also had a political impact on postwar reconstruction. Most of the war-shattered economies of Western Europe were heavily dependent on American loans and grants even before the announcement of the Marshall Plan by the United States Secretary of State in June 1947; thus, although the initiative in putting the Plan into operation was in theory given to the European governments concerned, the American government was bound to have a formative influence. In fact, although the Americans publicly offered advice and assistance, it appears that they also actively intervened to achieve an acceptable form both for the organisation which was to administer aid (OEEC) and for the level and type of aid to be granted. When the Schuman Plan of 1950 led to the initiation of a new phase in European economic integration, the Americans were firmly in favour; indeed, some groups in Congress were determined that only West European governments fully committed to integration efforts should be rewarded with Marshall Aid (a threat to Britain especially).

Although the United States government established and pursued an active presence in West European economic affairs during the early postwar years, its interest appeared to decline during the 1950s, perhaps as a result of the assumption that there was a strong consensus on the framework which had been established. During the negotiations which led up to the establishment of the EEC the American presence and voice were relatively unobtrusive, emerging only to ensure that the free trade area proposed by Britain did not pose a threat to the structures established by the Treaty of Rome. As already noted, the 1960s saw the beginning of a trend which associated both the United States and West European countries in the broader issues of global economic management. At the governmental level (with the assistance of the European Commission) it thus appeared that a *modus vivendi* had been established, however uneasily.

At another level – that of private investment and finance – the 1960s saw the beginning of a new 'invasion', led by the multinational corporations whose managers saw the opportunities offered by the integrated markets of the EEC. By this 'invasion' the character of the American presence in Western Europe was transformed: the military echelons of NATO and its associated hardware were joined by the multinational managers and the Eurodollar to an extent which was seen by some as threatening the stability of West European economic management. Just as the occupation forces had formed for some an alien implant in West European societies, and had brought penalties as well as benefits to their hosts, so the multinationals might be seen as a two-edged sword of modernisation and dependence. Whatever the merits of these arguments – and they will be revisited in Chapter 4 – the expansion of the American economic presence in Western Europe, and its privatisation after the primarily governmental involvement of the 1950s, fundamentally changed the setting of European–American relations. Given the level of American penetration in some West European industries, it became difficult to draw the line between what was properly 'European' and what 'American' in the balance-sheet of economic policy. In the changed economic conditions of the 1970s and 1980s this blurring of the boundaries between the United States and the societies of Western Europe was to create tensions – over the direction of government aid, the retention of investment and employment opportunities and the freedom of competition – which are still unresolved.

Associated at least in part with the military and economic presence already described, the postwar years also saw the establishment of an American social and cultural presence in Western Europe. By its nature, such a presence is difficult to define, although one of its characteristics has already been mentioned indirectly: the injection of American habits and expectations into West European societies still in the process of recovering their social and cultural identities. The impact of a confident and assertive American culture, expressed through film, television and other media and provided in an easily accessible form, brought both benefits and dangers – the benefit of provision for a growing and expectant mass audience, the danger of cultural dependency and the exhaustion of long-established traditions. At the same time, the penetration of American business and even tourists into Western Europe brought new habits of consumption and new forms of business practice into play, some of them by no means attuned to the established standards of the societies concerned. Reactions could be violent at times, and anti-Americanism in Gaullist France especially became a potent weapon in the hands of government during the 1960s, while during the 1970s the scandals caused by the activities of Lockheed and other American corporations bore witness to a continuing sensitivity.

Yet it was during the 1970s, in some key respects, that the balance changed. No longer was it simply the case that the Americans had established a presence – economic, military and social – in Western Europe. Increasingly, it appeared that Western European societies, governments and enterprises were able to fight back and to establish a growing presence in the United States. West European multinationals and financial institutions could expand with acquisitions, and threaten the position of American corporations; the production of mass entertainment and 'instant culture' was no longer the prerogative of the United States alone; and the loss of momentum and confidence in the American economy made a 'European revenge' possible as a sequel to the 'American challenge'. Both Western Europe and the United States, however, were ill-at-ease in the presence of the economic threat from Japan, which in key respects changed the setting in both America and West European societies, and posed a challenge to both. As in the Atlantic system, it appeared that initial certainty conveyed by American predominance had given way to a more even if uncertain balance as Western European economies recovered, and then to a situation in which the idea of a European–American balance itself was challenged.

The impact of changes in the American role on the prospects and progress of European social and economic development can thus hardly be overestimated, whether it has been benevolent or malign. In no sphere is this more clearly demonstrated than that of economic integration. During the 1950s and 1960s it was widely argued that the United States played the role of an 'external federator' with relation to the EEC; during the 1970s it appeared that Raymond Vernon's description of America as a 'rogue elephant in the forest' (1973) was far more appropriate. American inability to define or pursue consistent aims in the international economic field, whether the subject was energy, interest rates, or trade protection, came to be a central feature of the setting within which the European Communities struggled to survive; perhaps the most creative response produced by the EEC was the establishment of the European Monetary System (EMS) in 1978. The late 1970s and early 1980s saw an additional dimension of this problem, with the increasing use of economic sanctions as a weapon with which to punish offending regimes in Eastern Europe and elsewhere. This trend dragged the EEC willy-nilly into more highly politicised areas than ever before, with American pressure for controls on export of 'sensitive technologies' or the import of raw materials and energy coming up against the natural reluctance of West European governments to aggravate further the problems created by economic recession. President Reagan's attempts in 1981–2 to intervene in the transfer of technology and the export financing connected with the Siberian gas pipeline project made the most spectacular impact, but formed only part of a wider trend.

It can thus be concluded that Western Europe itself has formed a major arena for the interaction of the United States with West European societies and institutions. At this regional level the influence of the United States has been at times disruptive, at times supportive and at times simply unpredictable. Whatever its character, it has reflected the strength of the American presence within West European society in general and has generated strong feelings among national governments and the broader population of the region.

The Domestic Politics of European–American Relations

A final setting within which European–American relations have found their expression is that provided by the domestic political and social processes of the societies involved. As has already been suggested, European–American linkages constitute an area in which different national societies have 'got under each other's skins', and in which the contacts between those involved in political, economic and social life have been exceptionally close. This means that the ramifications of political processes within the various national societies involved might be expected to spread throughout the Euro-American system, and to affect in some degree the operation of the system as a whole. Changes in national moods in such conditions will have consequences beyond national boundaries, the fates of administrations and institutions will become connected, and the stability or legitimacy of national leaderships will be reflected in the broader climate of Atlantic relations. The evidence suggests that such features can indeed be identified, and that they have an important and growing bearing on the course of European–American relations.

Throughout the period since the Second World War it has been apparent that fluctuations in national mood and consensus have played a formative role in attitudes towards European–American relations, at both the elite and the popular levels. Perhaps the most dramatic and best-documented examples of this relationship have been gathered on the American side, where a great deal of attention is paid to the political 'temperature' of the country as a whole and of specific groups within society. In the immediate postwar period it was apparent that alongside the 'new internationalism' fostered by the war effort and the realisation of American strength, there still existed a powerful streak of isolationism and belief in 'fortress America'. This tension was manifested in the population at large, in Congress and even within the administrations of Roosevelt and Truman. In terms of the consolidation of links with Western Europe, it can be seen to have had a number of consequences, some of them of wider significance for the Cold War as a whole. First, it meant that the measures which needed to be taken (in the government's view) to maintain the security of Western Europe had to undergo scrutiny by a critical and sometimes openly hostile Congress, which was concerned to minimise obligations and to control material commitments. Secondly, and as a consequence of this first factor, the elaboration and institutionalisation of commitments was subject to very strict requirements; thus, for example, the checks on expenditure of Marshall Aid and military assistance were extensive and gave frequent opportunities for the reopening of controversial questions. Finally, the need to 'sell' alliance policies and European reconstruction to Congress and the people at large created a tendency for United States government leaders to emphasise the ideological and confrontational aspects of Cold War policies. Around such policies a powerful consensus was ultimately forged – one which espoused the cause of the Western Alliance and accepted the costs of European economic recovery, but also expected the West Europeans to play a full part in the securing of the free world.

To a large extent the story of American popular and elite attitudes towards Western Europe since the early 1950s reflects the consolidation and then the erosion of this Cold War consensus. In its heyday it accommodated the perversities of West European governments as long as they remained within the ideological pale, but in the early 1960s it was fractured by the disappointments which attended the idea of the Atlantic partnership, in the political field with the defection of the French and in the economic field with the challenge from the Common Market. This is not to discount a persistent and very powerful underlying disposition in favour of Western Europe; rather, it is to draw attention to the increasing differentiation which occurred within a broadly maintained consensus. By the end of the 1960s it was possible to identify powerful lobbies against the Common Agricultural Policy, in favour of a reduction in the level of American forces in Western Europe and against the European governments which showed less than total support for American policy in Vietnam. At the same time, however, the support for European integration as a platform for the activities of multinational business persisted, as did generalised support for NATO as a prop for American security.

The events of the early 1970s, however, clouded the picture still further: part of the Nixon–Kissinger foreign policy strategy called for the creation of a new consensus to give legitimacy to détente as a foreign policy programme, and while this was never fully established its pursuit entailed the fragmentation of the Cold War consensus. At the same time economic stagnation and the onset of recession created a host of parochial and special interest groups with axes to grind in the foreign policy arena. The fragmentation was compounded by the crises of Nixon's last year, the uncertainties of Gerald Ford and the ambivalent style of the Carter presidency. By 1978 it appeared possible to get a partial consensus on anything, and a generalised consensus on nothing, and Western Europe as a focus of American attitudes suffered accordingly. In the absence of a general rule about approaches to Western European countries, cases were fought on their merits and on the demands of the circumstances, taking into account difficulties with Congress and with parochial pressures. While the Reagan presidency promised to rectify this imbalance, with its pursuit of a new 'Cold War consensus', it was unable to do so, in fact; by 1982 the divisions and disputes in its foreign policies had reached epidemic proportions, and were reflected in a broader popular mood of confusion. The net result of this erosion and final destruction of consensus within the United States was to eliminate most of the assumptions and expectations which had (among other things) sustained the American approach to Western Europe, and to deprive policy-makers of any agreed groundrules for the formulation and conduct of policy. During 1983 there were signs of greater consistency at the governmental level, but it remained unclear how far this reflected a regeneration of the broader framework.

Whatever the complications of describing and analysing the political mood of American society, they pale into insignificance beside the task of interpreting West European attitudes and orientations. In itself, this is an indication of the ways in which these attitudes and orientations form a problematical element in European–American relations; after all, it has been all too easy for American policy-makers to discern a 'West European' mood or consensus, when such a phenomenon is bound to be elusive or non-existent among the populations of the dozen separate countries. Thus, any generalisations about the changing mood of Western Europe and its impact on European–American relations must be treated with extreme caution, but this does not rule out the possibility that some general and important trends can be identified, or that significant areas of divergence between countries can be given their due.

One important dimension of such an exercise is undoubtedly the tracing of feelings about national identity and national self-images in postwar Europe. From a position in the late 1940s where some societies were extremely ill-founded, and literally had to re-establish themselves along with their attendant political and economic systems, there emerged during the 1950s and 1960s a more confident and assertive mood in Western European countries. While this might be seen as the dominant trend – the French transition to Gaullism, and the West German and Italian recovery of economic and political self-esteem – there were exceptions, especially Britain, where the self-confidence of the early postwar period had given way to the stagnation and uncertainty of the 1960s. In a large degree, however, it could be argued that during the twenty years after the outbreak of the Korean War there had been a general strengthening of the societies of Western Europe, and a regeneration of national awareness and self-confidence.

It was to be expected that this process of regeneration would change national orientations towards the American presence in Western Europe, and towards the forces which legitimised the Western Alliance. Perhaps the least affected West European society was Britain, where an assumption that British foreign policy should pursue a global role was allied with a powerful belief in the Anglo-American 'special relationship'. At the other end of the spectrum the reassertion of French national autonomy, seen as submerged beneath a welter of imposed institutions and values, was dramatic; it might be argued that Gaullism and anti-Americanism were as much a sign of national vulnerability as of national self-confidence, but its impact was none the less spectacular at times. In West Germany the problem was rather different, since an intimate association with American needs and values was seen as the *sine qua non* of national security; what Willy Brandt called the 'self-recognition' of West Germans did not immediately imply the rejection of American values. Perhaps the least assertive of the major West European societies was Italy, where the absence of a positive orientation towards international affairs in general seems to have underlain the persistent acceptance of Atlantic values. Even such a sketchy review as this reveals the flimsy basis for any assumption of a European mood or consensus in the 1950s and 1960s, beyond the most general statements about national recovery and reconstruction.

During the 1970s, however, a number of factors coincided to make the West European popular mood into a major consideration for analysts of European–American relations. The first of these factors is one already mentioned in another context: the decline and collapse of the consensus in the United States which had sustained a particular set of attitudes towards the countries of Western Europe. Self-assertiveness in Western Europe and the growth of economic power within the context of the EEC had combined to create disillusionment, but this did not eliminate the necessity for trying to cultivate support for American policies. The difficulty was that it was even harder in the 1970s than in the 1960s to approach the problems of 'Western Europe' in a unified way, as Henry Kissinger discovered to his cost. Economic recession, particularly after the oil crisis of 1973–4, aggravated the problems of economic divergence which had already begun to dog the EEC in the 1960s, and produced naturally defensive reactions among West European populations.

International economic crises and dislocations underlined the tendency towards parochialism and protection.

At the same time interpretations of the security problems facing the Western Alliance were increasingly divergent, with the desire for a continued process of détente on the one hand offset by recognition of a persistent Soviet threat on the other. Crucially, this declining consensus on the security issue interacted with the fluctuations in American Cold War consensus to form a dominant motif of the domestic setting in many West European countries. When the Reagan administration attempted in the 1980s to encourage a new commitment to defence and security conceptions formed in the United States, it found itself confronted with a fragmented and often hostile West European audience. Nowhere was this more evident than in West Germany, where the burgeoning peace movements reflected a persistent yet sometimes muted tension between the desires on the one hand to demonstrate loyalty and solidarity with the Western Alliance, and on the other to promote reconciliation within Central Europe as a whole. The problem was broader, however, involving the continued relevance of Cold War axioms in Western Europe, and Europe more generally, and creating the possibility of far-reaching changes and instabilities.

It could thus be argued that the fluctuations of domestic mood and consensus on both sides of the Atlantic provide a crucial piece in the jigsaw of European–American relations. Such fluctuations, when combined with changes in the global arena, in the Atlantic system and the American presence within Western Europe itself, can be seen as formative influences in the problems faced by successive governments and administrations, both at home and abroad. In many ways they can also be said to have had implications for the stability and legitimacy of political systems and institutions in all of the countries involved, and thus to have challenged another of the assumptions in which European–American relations have been thought to rest.

From the early years of the Cold War it was almost taken as axiomatic that, despite their very different histories, traditions and practices, the regimes of Western Europe and the United States shared some basic affinities and a degree of mutual responsiveness which could be relied upon to buttress transatlantic co-operation. In fact, as already noted, United States governments bent considerable efforts towards ensuring that the embryonic political systems of much of postwar Western Europe coincided with their preferences and prejudices. 'Atlanticism' in general can be seen to have rested on preferences for parliamentary democracy, for evolutionary change and for a climate of political stability. Through the 1950s and 1960s on the whole these preferences were satisfied, although the nature of political change in the French 4th Republic and the presidential regime established by de Gaulle can be seen as discomfiting or disturbing factors. In addition, the cultivation of bureaucratic links between the United States and West European administrations, whether through the institutional channels provided by NATO and the OEEC/OECD or through less formal contacts, enhanced the mutual understanding and respect felt on all sides. Sometimes, admittedly, this could lead to mistaken assumptions and unexpected disappointments, such as those attending the Suez crisis, the MLF, or British attempts to enter the EEC; but on the whole, and again with qualifications in the case of France, the bureaucratic substructure of Atlanticism prospered along with a political convergence which was partly assumed and partly contrived.

The later 1960s and the 1970s witnessed significant challenges to these assumptions, however. On the one side, the nature of political change in the United States and West European countries undermined the assumptions of convergence and of stability which had only been slightly shaken by events in France; while on the other hand, there emerged challenges to the legitimacy of incumbent regimes and political arrangements which had an equally unsettling effect. Quite apart from the self-conscious separatism of Gaullist France, it became less easy as time went on to take a commitment to 'Western democracy' as read in the affairs of some West European countries. There had always been difficulties with Portugal and Spain (the latter effectively being excluded from NATO as a result); in the mid-1960s the installation of a military regime in Greece further stretched the definition. Although the Greek colonels left the scene in 1974 (partly as the result of a war with Turkey over Cyprus which further stretched the fabric of the Western Alliance), there emerged in the mid-1970s a seemingly more far-reaching threat to the democratic process in several West European societies: that of Eurocommunism. The origins of this phenomenon were diverse: in Portugal it emerged as part of a revolutionary upheaval following the downfall of the Caetano regime; in Spain it was part of the political ferment created by the death of Franco and the re-establishment of democracy; in Italy it took the shape of a projected 'historic compromise' between the declining forces of the Christian Democrats and the Italian Communist Party (PCI); and in France it found expression through the union of mainstream Socialists and the French Communist Party (PCF), with the aim of maximising the electoral impact of each. Whatever its origins, it appeared at the time that the possibility of communists holding office in major West European governments posed a fundamental threat to the ideological and institutional convergence which had sustained the Western Alliance, and thus that domestic political change might have profound international effects. By 1981, however, it appeared that the ghost had been well and truly laid, with the emergence of moderate regimes in Portugal and Spain, the seemingly indefinite postponement of the 'historic compromise' and the defeat of the PCF in the 1981 French elections.

It was not only in Western Europe, however, that challenges to the established order emerged. In the United States the growth of the 'imperial presidency' based on the Executive's domination of national security policy in particular foretold a growing imbalance between the branches of government, exacerbated by popular discontent at the impact of the Vietnam War. Matters came to a head in the early 1970s when the Nixon government first instigated a major unannounced extension of the Vietnam War into Cambodia, and then was caught out in its misuse of Executive powers during the 1972 election campaign (the so-called 'Watergate' incident). The result was a crisis for the legitimacy of the presidency, and an enduring instability in the balance between President and Congress. Gerald Ford, Jimmy Carter and Ronald Reagan alike were unable to manufacture a position of pre-eminence akin to that enjoyed by the presidents of the 1960s, while Congress proved at times incapable of handling its newly acquired resources and prestige. To this confusion was added another: the increasing evidence of bureaucratic conflicts and fragmentation within successive administrations, which often produced conflicting 'foreign policies' emanating from different departments, and occasionally prevented the emergence of any policy at all.

Some of the consequences of this development for European–American relations have already been charted: the loss of confidence and consensus in the United States, the reluctance to pronounce upon or accept responsibility for affairs in the international system at large. The implications were the more profound, it could be argued, because this loss of direction in the United States coincided with a more general erosion of the legitimacy of government throughout the Euro-American system. In the recession-dominated 1970s the capacity of governments to satisfy their citizens' needs at home and abroad appeared severely limited, and whereas in the 1950s a similar feeling had helped to give rise to the EEC, this time the future of European integration itself seemed in jeopardy as a result of the failure to resolve problems of employment, inflation and raw materials supplies. In addition to being built on assumptions about political and ideological convergence, European–American relations had also taken for granted certain standards of governmental performance, in the economic and social spheres, which now began to appear unrealistic.

In such circumstances the task confronting national leaderships and elites within the setting of both domestic and international demands was daunting, to say the least. It has always been a feature of European–American relations that contacts between national leaders and elite groups have been intense and frequent: during the early Cold War years the influence of Monnet and others on the course of transatlantic relations was profound, just as were the effects of mutual hostility and recriminations during the years of Kennedy and de Gaulle. During the 1970s and 1980s, however, the nature of such contacts became extremely paradoxical. On the one hand, the frequency and formality with which leaders met increased, as a result of economic summits and the growing emphasis on personal diplomacy. On the other hand, however, leaders preoccupied with their own domestic insecurities and concerned to protect demonstrably vulnerable economies were less inclined to form the kind of close working relationships which had characterised earlier phases of European–American dealings. To be sure, there had been difficulties and periods of personal rancour many times before; now, however, the combination of national preoccupations and domestic political insecurities produced a new mood of indifference and hard-nosed realism on all sides, which even the substructure of bureaucratic contacts could not mitigate.

It might be possible to conclude from the arguments in this chapter that European-American relations, or the 'Euro–American system', have effectively disappeared into the broader setting of international affairs, and become subject to the general laws of world politics. Such a claim would be at once untrue and unwise. European–American relations, as is apparent, are rich in their implications for the international system, and distinctive in the number of levels at which they can be identified or formed. What this chapter does reveal is the way in which the various elements of European–American relations have been transformed over the period since 1945. The coexistence of changes within the global, Atlantic, West European and domestic arenas has posed continuing problems for policy-makers and analysts. Sometimes the changes have been mutually reinforcing and converging, more often as time has passed they have become divergent and perverse in their implications, accentuating the uncertainties and unpredictability of the context within which European–American relations have persisted. Here the concern has been mainly with identifying the elements of the context; in Chapter 4 the focus shifts to the substance of European–American relations and the issues on which they have centred.

Further Reading

The following references are listed in accordance with the division of material in the chapter. Many of these studies contain material of interest in more than one of the 'settings' on which the chapter centres; the inclusion of an item in one section rather than others indicates that it has particularly interesting points to make about the area concerned, not that it has nothing to say about others.

The global arena: On the changing nature of East–West relations and their impact on European–American links see, for example: Alting von Geusau (1983); Brzezinski (1965); DePorte (1979); Etzold and Gaddis (1978); and Wolfers (1964). Major phases in American policy can be identified in: Chace and Ravenal (1976); Cromwell (1978); Hoffmann (1968, 1978) (especially useful for the contrasts between the two sets of evaluations); and Osgood (1968). The impact on Western Europe (particularly the EEC) can be seen from: Feld (1978); and Grosser (1980). Many of the more recent of those cited here also point to the 'new globalism' and its impact on European–American relations; but see also Freedman (1982).

The Atlantic system: The following are particularly useful in charting the shifting foundations of 'Atlanticism': Art (1982); Beloff (1976); Calleo and Rowland (1973); Goodman (1975); Hahn and Pfaltzgraff (1979); and Kaiser and Schwartz (1977). On specific areas and episodes see, for example: Ball (1982) and Monnet (1978), who say a great deal about the elite ties which sustained much of the Atlantic system's early life; Fox and Schilling (1973), who cover the 'strategic gap' of the late 1960s; Hanrieder (1974), a collection which reflects the mid-1970s crisis; Nau (1971) on the 'technology gap'; Rosecrance (1976) on the idea of the United States as an 'ordinary country'; and Pfaltzgraff (1975) on the new challenge of Japan.

Western Europe: The growth of the American 'presence' is dealt with in many of the general texts, for example: Grosser (1980); and Serfaty (1979). More specifically, see: Harrison (1974); Layton (1968); Newhouse (1971); Schilling *et al.* (1973); and Vernon (1971). Changes in the role of the United States are dealt with in (among others): van der Beugel (1966); Calleo (1970); Camps (1967); Rosecrance (1976); and Vernon (1973). The European response can be sampled from: Calleo (1965); Chace and Ravenal (1976, esp. chapter by Hoffmann); Diebold (1960); Hoffmann (1964–5); and Servan-Schreiber (1968).

Domestic politics: The following have a strong focus on the domestic dimensions of European–American relations: Grosser (1980, lots of detail); Landes (1977, esp. on Eurocommunism); Osgood *et al.* (1973); Oye *et al.* (1979, esp. on the American mood in 1970s); Richardson (1966); Serfaty (1979); Storey (1981); Vannicelli (1974); Webb (1979); and Willis (1968, 1971). There is also a useful comparative treatment by Nicholas Wahl in Chace and Ravenal (1976).

4 Issues: the Substance of European–American Relations

In Chapter 3 the focus of the discussion was primarily upon the environment within which European–American relations have emerged and have developed over the period since the end of the Second World War. It was argued at the beginning of that chapter that a lot can be learned about relationships such as those between the societies of Western Europe and the United States by examining the ways in which environmental factors can operate to influence or constrain social action. In the course of the discussion it became apparent that given the complexity and indeterminate nature of the setting within which European–American relations have been carried on, the problem of coping with fluctuations and interconnections between environmental forces was a daunting one. The present chapter is designed to carry the argument further, by concentrating on a second element in the Euro-American system: the substantive issues around which actions and interactions have taken place. Writers on international relations have increasingly used the concept of an 'issue-area' to discuss the ways in which the goals, activities and interactions of states or other groupings produce clusters of particularly intense collaboration or competition. Others have preferred to talk and write in terms of the 'agenda' of international concerns, and the ways in which certain 'agenda items' become matters of special importance or political significance. Here the focus is in many ways a combination of the two approaches, with the aim of defining those issues which have consistently been at the centre of European–American relations, and of assessing the ways in which their salience and significance have fluctuated.

The literature on European–American relations – and the concerns of policy-makers – have generally identified three 'agenda items' as lying at the core of the relationship. First, it has been plain that the assumed strategic unity of Western Europe and the United States, expressed in its most tangible form by the North Atlantic Treaty Organisation (NATO), has been accorded major significance by both academics and policy-makers. While the significance of NATO has been uncontested, however, the underlying assumptions of the Alliance, its strategic orientation and its operational effectiveness have been a continued source of debate and questioning. The same has been true in different ways of a second major issue-area: the economic fabric of European–American relations, and the construction and demise of the postwar economic order. It has already been noted that the framework of economic activity in the Atlantic area and beyond was a growing source of uncertainty during the postwar period, and the major symptoms of this uncertainty have attracted substantial attention and debate. Both the economic debate and the strategic climate of European–American relations have been related to a third set of issues, those which have arisen from the evolution of political forces within Europe and the wider world, and which have led to controversies about the nature of East–West relations and the respective roles of Western European countries and the United States. An exploration of these three areas will reveal not only the ways in which the issues have evolved and the agenda has changed, but also the ways in which they coexist and overlap, often with profound consequences.

Strategy: the Limits of Alliance

It has often been argued that whatever else might be problematic in European–American relations, the Alliance (NATO) is not – that the underlying solidarity of the North Atlantic countries in the face of an identifiable and persistent threat has held firm throughout the period since 1949 (when the North Atlantic Treaty was signed). As was noted in Chapter 2, this assumption is central to explanations of the Euro-American system which focus on its core of concerns with power and security. In order to test this assumption, and to explore the strategic issues which have emerged in European–American relations, it makes sense first of all to examine the nature of the Alliance on which they all ultimately centre. What kind of alliance is NATO? And what has been its relationship to the changing setting discussed in Chapter 3?

One immediately striking feature of NATO is its persistence and longevity – some observers have been led to describe it as a 'permanent alliance', in the belief that in so far as anything can be predicted in the international system, the demand for something like NATO can be foreseen for many years ahead. In more formal terms, the North Atlantic Treaty constitutes an arrangement for collective defence on a regional basis, as provided for in Article 51 of the United Nations Charter, and is focused on a defined geographical area bounded by the countries of North America and Western Europe (including parts of Scandinavia and the Mediterranean). Within this area the allies undertake to assist any of the members who may become subject to aggression, and to prepare for such events through a process of continual self-help and mutual assistance. The Alliance is not simply a military arrangement, however – the members pledge themselves to defend and promote democratic values and ideas, among other things – nor is its implementation a purely mechanical or automatic process, since the members are free to decide on how best to fulfil their obligations. One important consideration in this process is likely to be the allies' perceptions of a common threat, and thus a shared interest in upholding their commitments; although the North Atlantic Treaty itself was rapidly complemented by a sophisticated political and military structure (NATO) which spends a great deal of time planning for co-ordinated military action, it must be remembered that in the final analysis the member-governments have the responsibility for fulfilling the provisions of the Alliance. In this sense, NATO is an extraordinary form of something which has been a central mechanism of international politics for centuries – an alliance aimed at parrying a perceived threat within the context of a balance of international power.

The form of NATO as an alliance is made more distinctive still by its geopolitical make-up. Although alliances have been made and have persisted between geographically distant countries before, a military coalition between groups of countries separated by 3,000 miles of North Atlantic, with all its implications for logistic and tactical collaboration, is fraught with potential dangers. As was noted in Chapter 1, the creation of the North Atlantic Treaty was at least in part the work of West European governments anxious for reassurance that the North American allies would not retreat from involvement in the affairs of the Old World. The anxiety was compounded by the fact that the United States was the world's dominant military power, and by the recognition that without an American guarantee there was a real danger of either Soviet expansion or German *revanchism*, or both. In order to establish the credibility of defence arrangements for Western Europe, it was necessary to bind the United States to the postwar status quo, and if possible to make sure that there were tangible signs of continuing American commitment. On the American side, given the ambivalence already noted about the appropriate role for the United States in the international system, and the additional complications of domestic political alignments, the Treaty (and later the Organisation) had to be sold as a concrete defence against a global threat, and not simply a unilateral American pledge. The process was made easier by evidence of a mounting threat not only in Europe (the Berlin blockade and the communist coup in Czechoslovakia during 1948), but also in the Far East and Indochina (the Korean War and the French problems in Vietnam).

From this brief sketch of NATO's origins and features, it can be seen not only that it has been a remarkably resilient and elaborate alliance system, but also that it contains the seeds of important contradictions. It is an alliance of equal members, but with one dominant member; it is an alliance based on a multilateral and mutual guarantee, which depends crucially upon the guarantee sustained by one member. Although it contains elements of integration and collaboration which could almost be described as supranational, it gives the last word to the perceptions and actions of national governments. At the same time as it focuses on a quite clearly defined geographical area, it has also been presented as the keystone in a broader defence against a general threat. The threat can be defined in strictly military terms, but has also acquired strong ideological, political and economic overtones. As a result of these ambiguities, which have been given greater force by changes in the broader environment of European–American relations, the evolution of NATO has been accompanied by continued and often acrimonious debate about what might be termed the 'limits of alliance': the perception of threat and the extent of the allies' obligations, the sharing of the military and economic burden, and the geographical or functional scope of the alliance's operations.

During the late 1940s and the early 1950s it was relatively easy to define the origins and intensity of the threat faced by the NATO allies: a Soviet attack in massive strength through the centre of Europe, against which the weakened powers of Western Europe would be powerless to defend themselves from their own resources. The need was thus for defence, and for defence of a relatively novel kind based on novel types of commitments. In essence, the arrangements which emerged involved a guarantee by a geographically distant country – the United States – that it would maintain a presence in Western Europe, and that it would assist other members of NATO when they came under attack not only through deployment of forces in being, but also by reinforcement and by the use of its nuclear monopoly. The American commitment was the *sine qua non* of the Alliance, and rapidly came to be expressed in American domination of the military structures established in NATO; the first Supreme Allied Commander Europe (SACEUR) was an American (Eisenhower), as have been all subsequent holders of this post. Although the British were given a few of the NATO commands, and the French got one, it was clear to all concerned that the Americans dominated, and that this was the logical concomitant of their nuclear and conventional guarantees.

Two effects of this leadership and of its structural embodiment in NATO were to become apparent. First, it meant that as the United States expanded its global involvement, acquiring new allies and clients by a process sometimes described as 'pactomania', there emerged doubts about the level and extent of its commitment to the defence of Western Europe, especially if this involved a major (and expensive) conventional presence there. Secondly, it meant that some of the European members of NATO found their political recovery and expectations unsatisfied by their structural subordination in the Alliance; this particularly affected the

French, who were later to make it a prime motivation for demanding structural reform and threatening defection.

The rationale for the Alliance and for its members' commitments was further tested by the development of the political climate in the international system at large, and especially in relations between the United States and the Soviet Union. As the threat of direct and immediate Soviet aggression receded – partly, of course, as a reflection of NATO's consolidation – and as direct communication between Washington and Moscow developed, the allies became concerned with a triple threat from the Americans themselves. The first part of this threat was globalism – the already noted distraction of American policy-makers by events in distant arenas which threatened to dilute their commitment to NATO. A second threat came from unilateralism – the temptation for the American leadership to conceive of the problems of the world, and of Europe in particular, as a concern for themselves in direct dialogue with the Soviet Union. As with globalism, the danger was that the West European allies would be neglected, that consultation would be conveniently forgotten and that NATO would be put aside in the search for broader change. A third danger was rather different, and consisted of the possibility that the United States structural domination of the Alliance would lead to interventionism, the attempt to manipulate strategic attitudes within Western Europe to fit in with a particular conception of the Alliance. In one form or another, this three-pronged threat from the United States has played a central part in the evolution of NATO since the early 1950s.

In the late 1950s and early 1960s the interaction of the structural properties of the Alliance with the recovery of the major West European countries, and the growing globalism of American policy, brought about an open confrontation which called into question the underlying assumptions of Alliance unity and obligations. One of the first acts of the Gaullist regime in France after its accession to power in 1958 was a call for a kind of tripartite 'directorate' to run NATO and to co-ordinate its approach to a broad range of issues within Europe and elsewhere. This attempt to dilute what de Gaulle saw as an Anglo-Saxon monopoly was spurned – but the issue was inflamed further by the Kennedy administration's calls for a kind of 'Atlantic partnership' which seemed designed to perpetuate the United States dominance in NATO's inner councils, and by the apparent resuscitation of the Anglo-American 'special relationship' in the early 1960s. Emboldened by what they saw as a relaxation of tensions in the global arena, the French persisted in challenging American plans for the Alliance, such as the ill-fated Multilateral Force (MLF), and eventually, in 1966, de Gaulle announced their withdrawal from the integrated military command structure (not from the Alliance *per se*). At the same time, he pursued a policy aimed at a kind of 'détente' with Eastern Europe and the Soviet Union, and called for a Europe united 'from the Atlantic to the Urals'.

The Gaullist belief that alliances were reflections of temporary coincidences of national interest rather than permanent structures was clearly a pragmatic response to French aspirations as well as an ideological doctrine, but none the less it posed a challenge to the rationale of NATO as a whole. Partly as a result, other European allies during the late 1960s found themselves a form of organisation which began to establish their distinctive needs within the Alliance, and which was eventually formalised in the so-called Eurogroup. During the early 1970s the West Europeans within NATO also found more of an independent role in the negotiations for Mutual and Balanced Force Reductions (MBFR) which began in Vienna in 1973, and in the Conference on Security and Co-operation in Europe which produced the 1975 Helsinki Declaration. Both of these sets of negotiations persisted into the 1980s, with no sign of final resolution, but with continuing active participation by West European members of NATO.

At the same time, however, the threats of American globalism, unilateralism and interventionism periodically re-emerged. The whole process of détente raised the possibility of deals being concluded between the United States and the Soviet Union (for example, on nuclear weapons) without the European allies being able to influence the bargaining process. Paradoxically, the decline of détente and the emergence of greater tensions between the United States and the Soviet Union in areas outside Europe created a similar danger, with the possibility that American responses to perceived Soviet expansionism would put the NATO allies in an untenable position. From the October War in the Middle East during 1973 to the crises over Iran, Afghanistan and Poland in the 1980s, it was plain that the American tendency to impose responses on West European members of the Alliance, or to assume their acquiescence in often risky ventures, was still a factor to be reckoned with, despite the renewed consensus on the existence of a growing Soviet threat. Quite simply, it often appeared that West European and American views of their obligations – moral or material – were at odds, and that this reflected fundamental tensions in the Alliance: was NATO a concert of free nations or a protectorate, a coalition with a common purpose or a façade for a sphere of influence dominated by an increasingly feeble and capricious superpower?

Associated with the problem of Alliance obligations has been that of 'burden-sharing'. In the nuclear age, and the era of sophisticated 'conventional' weapons systems, alliances can be expensive, and NATO is perhaps the most expensive of all. This adds a new gloss to what has always been a problem with international alliances – the difficulties of sharing the costs and benefits equitably. NATO's early years were less problematical in this respect, simply because it appeared clear that many of the West European members were incapable of providing adequately for their own defence. It was not long, however, before the pressures of peacetime politics in the United States and the evident economic recovery of several major West European societies created fertile ground for controversy. In essence, the American desire to multilateralise the burden of conventional defence in Western Europe came up against the unwillingness or incapacity of West European governments; at the same time, those governments counted upon the perpetuation of an American military presence, and especially on the American nuclear guarantee, to ensure their ultimate security. Matters were not improved by American domination of the market for conventional arms, which led European members of the Alliance to complain that they paid dearly in commercial terms for the American guarantee.

It is at this point – in the relationship between the nuclear and conventional burdens assumed by the members of NATO – that the Alliance's most distinctive feature comes into play. NATO was the first, and arguably is the only, 'nuclear alliance', centred on collective defence through the use of fission or (later) fusion weapons, yet from this basic quality flow a number of paradoxes felt very directly in the field of burden-sharing. In the earliest years of NATO the American nuclear supremacy over the Soviet Union and the demands of economic reconstruction on both sides of the Atlantic combined to make a doctrine of 'massive retaliation' attractive to American policy-makers and European allies alike. As Soviet nuclear capacity grew during the 1950s the promise that any attack on NATO territory would be met with an American nuclear response began to appear less attractive: West European allies, especially the West Germans, recognised that they might well suffer immense damage in the course of being defended, and American strategists realised that a more sophisticated and controlled response was needed if the Soviets were effectively to be deterred.

Thus, it was that in the early 1960s the United States adopted the so-called 'flexible response' doctrine – a doctrine which despite attacks and adaptations still forms the core of NATO nuclear strategy. The idea of 'flexible response' implies an ability to meet and match a threat at any level, and to control with great precision the use of both conventional and nuclear techniques. Implicit in the doctrine is a great centralisation of military planning and decision-making, and a re-emphasis of the role of conventional forces: in addition, there is the possibility either of an extended conventional war or of a nuclear war, fought at the 'tactical', 'battlefield', or 'theatre' level, which does not escalate to a strategic nuclear exchange. For West European leaderships, over the years since 1960 great dilemmas have been created by the pursuit of this doctrine, and a variety of responses has been in evidence. At one end of the spectrum, the French have generally chosen to stress their nuclear independence, at great cost to themselves, by developing a medium-range nuclear force which (it is claimed) constitutes an effective if minimal deterrent. The British have adopted a line which relies upon a national deterrent force but only envisages its use in close collaboration with the Alliance (and thus with the United States). For the West Germans, however, the dilemma has been the most serious: forbidden to manufacture nuclear weapons by the terms of their membership in NATO, they have sought to maximise American commitment and to bear the burden in terms of conventional forces or by allowing the stationing of large numbers of nuclear weapons on their territory.

This brief and crude review of the problem for West European governments shows the extent of their predicament, given the fluctuations of American enthusiasm and doctrinal orientation. At various times the European allies have feared that American willingness to bear the burden will wane, and that they may be abandoned to their fate; at others, they have felt that the price of American guarantees may be the wasting of Central and Western Europe in a war which does not damage the American homeland. The American response to this dilemma has not always been surefooted, influenced as it has been by the needs of superpower relations, the economic and other pressures at home, and the designs of nuclear strategists. Thus, the attempt to devolve some responsibility to Europeans in the nuclear field through devices such as the MLF was unsuccessful in the 1960s, while the arms control elements of détente with the Soviet Union raised new fears in Bonn and other European capitals during the early 1970s.

Greater and more continuous tensions, however, emerged in the mid-1970s, when pressures grew for an enhancement of intermediate-range (or theatre) nuclear forces in Europe to counter Soviet deployment of weapons such as the SS-20 missile system. On the one hand, West Germans and other leaderships wanted the reassurance of an expanded American presence in the shape of Cruise and Pershing II systems; on the other hand, popular opposition, and the fear that nuclear war could now be confined to Europe more surely than before, created widespread ambivalence and a demand for new arms control negotiations. American responses under the Reagan administration were often less than conciliatory, calling for the allies to play their part and raising the spectre of troop withdrawals. As had been the case since its inception, the questions 'what is NATO for?' and 'who is it for?' refused to submit to easy answers.

If NATO is conceived as the provider of a 'collective good' – security or deterrence – then it is clear from what has just been said that from its earliest years the burden of providing this good has been unequally distributed. At the same time the good itself has been enjoyed by societies whether or not they have contributed in appropriate measure to its provision. In the language of collective goods theory, there have been a number of 'free riders' (or at least riders receiving a substantial discount) in the Alliance, and part of American policy has been aimed at reducing their privileges. There is, as always, another side to the story; in this case, it would stress the benefits of political control and access which have been purchased by the American contributions, quite apart from any gains in security. Whichever view is taken, it is clear that the problems of sustaining the Alliance by paying in cash or in political support have been continuous. The 1960s witnessed the MLF controversy and the ascendancy of 'flexible response' ideas which stressed the need for conventional support to the (American) nuclear guarantee; the 1970s saw almost continual pressures upon the European allies to beef up their conventional forces, at the same time as those allies professed continuing doubts about both the need for an upgrading of their forces and the requirement for ever-larger numbers of American nuclear forces stationed on their territory. The impact of economic recession only served to exacerbate mutual doubts and suspicions arising from the fundamentally asymmetric nature of the Alliance itself.

The limits of NATO as an alliance have thus been tested almost continuously since its establishment, both by the divergent perceptions of members as to their obligations and privileges and by the problem of burden-sharing. If NATO is seen as a club for those desiring international security, then there has been no time at which the club's constitution, its rules of procedure and its subscription have not been in dispute. In the same way, there have been frequent tensions centreing on the area of applicability of the Alliance – a general problem to which there are several distinct aspects. First, although the geographical scope of the Alliance seems well defined, there have been periodic efforts to modify the definition and to include areas of special interest or value to members. One of these was achieved at an early stage, with the inclusion in the North Atlantic Treaty of the Algerian departments of France; others followed in the shape of extension of membership to Greece and Turkey during the early 1950s. For a time it appeared that NATO might become the core of a global alliance system, as the Soviet and associated threats were defined in ever more expansive terms. After all, the stimulus to institutionalisation of NATO itself had been rooted outside Europe – in Korea – and there was a widespread appreciation that the communist threat was growing in Asia especially.

Appearances were deceptive, however, and much of the period since the early 1950s has been spent in drawing limits to the geographical scope of NATO rather than extending it. Even the traumatic process of incorporating West Germany into the Alliance can be seen as formalising a boundary which had already been accepted as essential to the Alliance, although clearly it had the effect of transforming West Germany from a passive recipient of protection into an increasingly active contributor to the common defence. Likewise, the incorporation of Spain in 1982 did little to alter the prevailing conception of NATO's applicability, although it did import a number of additional causes of tension into the Organisation in the shape of the dispute over Gibraltar and some North African conflicts. The defections – of France from the integrated command in 1966, and of Greece in 1975, partly as a result of the war with Turkey over Cyprus – have had little effective impact on the defence commitments of other members. More intriguing – and sometimes dramatic – have been attempts to establish a requirement for Alliance support or solidarity in conflicts which by common consent fall outside its area of applicability. Thus, the French in the mid-1950s tried to gather NATO assistance for their civil war in Algeria, with remarkably little success (indeed, this has been seen as one of the contributory factors to the later Gaullist confrontation with the 'Anglo-Saxons'). On a much grander scale was the attempt by the British and French in 1956 to present their invasion of the Suez Canal zone as an operation worthy of NATO endorsement: the Americans took a very firm line in opposition to any such use of force. Such a stance was heavy with irony in the light of the Americans' later attempts to harness NATO to their activities first in Vietnam and later in the Middle East. The response of European allies in the first of these cases was querulous, to say the least, despite earnest American efforts to gather token contributions to the campaign. In the second case, especially during the 1973 October War, American indignation at European faint-heartedness reached a peak – Henry Kissinger was quoted as accusing the Europeans of acting as if the Alliance did not exist after they had objected to American use of NATO airfields in the operation to resupply Israel.

Assumptions of Alliance solidarity in far-flung areas have thus come up against some severe limitations in areas from the Middle East to South-East Asia. In addition to these purely geographical limitations, however, there have also emerged what might be described as functional limitations to the applicability of the Alliance; in other words, boundaries drawn to delineate the range of acceptable methods through which NATO's objectives (or those of members) can be pursued. NATO, after all, is a military alliance and possesses a quite elaborate mechanism for ensuring military co-operation; even in the military sphere the members have often been far from wholly united on the issue of methods. Outside the military arena there is even more confusion, often because very little is said in the Treaty about non-military methods of achieving security. During the 1970s and 1980s, it has been argued, non-military forms of sanctions, resources and punishments have been far more salient to policy-makers given the disutilities which are seen as attending the use of military force. The result of this increasing focus on non-military sanctions for an alliance such as NATO is likely to be a series of conflicts and tensions over acceptable methods. Such tensions are not unprecedented; from the early days of NATO there were differences of view between members over the application of strategic embargoes and diplomatic sanctions.

The early 1980s, however, saw a proliferation of financial and economic sanctions which had the effect of highlighting underlying confusions over the appropriate methods with which to ensure security or punish an adversary. American actions against Iran, against the Soviet Union after its invasion of Afghanistan in 1980 and against the Soviets again after the imposition of martial law in Poland during 1981 placed an unprecedented burden on Alliance solidarity because they demanded a co-ordinated response against something less than a direct military threat and with something less than military means, thus creating a much more complex and indeterminate calculus for all of the allies. There was less uncertainty and ambivalence about NATO attitudes to American involvement in El Salvador, or the British expedition to recover the Falkland Islands from Argentina, primarily because the stakes were lower; but the atmosphere of recriminations and hostility created by actions against the Soviet Union in particular revealed just how far the Alliance had moved from the early Cold War years.

Economic Issues: Recovery, Rivalry and Recession

At the same time as the consolidation and institutionalisation of NATO was taking place, during the period 1949–55, there emerged in European–American relations what could almost be described as an economic alliance – a set of structures, agreements and practices which formed a parallel to the assumed affinities of Western European countries and the United States in the strategic sphere. The Marshall Plan was only the most dramatic move in the process which led to an intense and closely co-ordinated set of interactions, and which led many to believe that a kind of 'permanent alliance' could persist between the industrialised market economies of the North Atlantic area. As noted in Chapters 2 and 3, it was often argued that increasing interdependence and mutual sensitivities would form an ever-growing basis for common responses to shared problems, to the ultimate benefit of all concerned. By the 1980s, however, such hopes or expectations seemed much less securely founded, and part of the explanation can be seen to lie in the characteristics of the 'alliance' which earlier had seemed so stable.

Just as the North Atlantic Treaty – and later NATO – had arisen out of the perception of a common threat on both sides of the Atlantic, so it could be said that the emerging 'economic alliance' represented a response to dangers in the economic and social spheres. Although Marshall's speech announcing American aid for European economic recovery was couched in general terms, it became clear that defence of the market economy and promotion of an 'open' system of exchange and payments was central to America's strategy. This was not simply a response to a perceived threat from communist parties or their sympathisers: it had its roots also in fears of a return to the 'beggar-thy-neighbour' strategies of the 1930s. It depended not only on the erection of a series of international institutions – chief among them the General Agreement on Tariffs and Trade (GATT) and the International Monetary Fund (IMF) – but also on the preservation of relatively 'open' market economies at the national level. In the case of Western Europe these structures were supplemented and given additional force by the material assistance available through the Marshall Plan and the European Recovery Programme. Thus, as in the case of NATO, the parties were subject to certain demands for co-ordinated action, and were provided with a number of incentives to adhere to the practices of the 'alliance'.

The 'balance of power' in this economic 'alliance' was as lopsided in many ways as was the balance in the strategic sphere, with the American economy in a position of almost complete dominance, the dollar in great demand as a medium of exchange, and the products of American industry and agriculture needed to satisfy the requirements of West European reconstruction. Although the British especially (through Keynes and others) had played a great role in formulating the basis for the postwar economic order among industrial countries, the United States alone had the capacity to get the system working. This also enabled the Americans to define some of the boundaries of the system: from an early stage it was clear that two areas of activity were central – the monetary and trade sectors – and that the benefits were likely to be confined to those who at least in principle accepted the assumptions of a 'liberal' or 'open' economy at the national and international level.

By the mid-1950s, therefore, it could be argued that the basis of an 'open' world economy had been established in the North Atlantic area, providing benefits for all concerned in the shape of economic security and stability. As in the case of NATO, an extraordinary form of historical phenomenon – the creation of an economic 'sphere of influence' under the aegis of a major power – had emerged and been consolidated. Just as in the NATO case, however, the situation contained a number of inherent tensions and ambiguities which were to plague the 'alliance' almost from its inception. It was an 'open' system among theoretically equal economies, but with one dominant economy and several which had to espouse protectionism in order to survive. It demanded of its members that they gave priority to the maintenance of a certain kind of international order, sometimes at the expense of pursuing domestic practices which demanded modifications to the 'rules'. It was focused on limited areas of activity – trade and payments – in a relatively limited geographical area, but was seen as the prototype for a global system encompassing all areas of economic activity. Not surprisingly, therefore, the development of this 'alliance' was accompanied by disputes and conflicts over the terms of membership and the application of rules. In the economic as opposed to the strategic sphere, however, a distinctive quality was given to these problems by the dynamic effects of European recovery and the very 'openness' of the hoped-for system.

The question of the obligations and commitments entailed in membership of the postwar economic regime was opened up at a very early stage. In one sense the shape of the system itself – excluding the centralised economies of Eastern Europe and the Soviet Union – reflected a decision to set the terms in such a way as to prevent 'deviant' members from enjoying the resources available. But there were quite significant disagreements even among those who did accept the 'terms of entry'. One cause of such disagreements was the process of reconstruction in Western Europe itself, since it became evident at an early stage that the requirements of currency convertibility and a non-discriminatory trading system were at odds with the need for recovery. Thus, attempts by the British and others to comply with the convertibility requirement were shown to be premature, while the necessity for continuing quantitative and qualitative trade restrictions was reflected in trade policies pursued by the French and others. Further disagreements emerged over the shape of economic organisations in West European societies, where there were diverse views on the extent of state intervention in the economy: only in West Germany was there a really full-blown adherence to the forms implied in American assumptions. The beginnings of European economic integration, embodied in the Schuman Plan and ECSC, raised further doubts in the United States about the acceptable level of deviation from the market economy and non-discrimination, but the assumed political benefits of stability in the coal and steel sectors, and the fact that no other solution to the Franco-German problem presented itself were sufficient to override continuing suspicions.

With the gradual elimination of trade restrictions and the eventual restoration of convertibility in the late 1950s, the consensus on the obligations of membership in the European–American economic regime appeared to gain strength. It was still apparent, however, that the issue of trade discrimination was being postponed against the promise of future political benefits. The EEC had about it a number of explicitly discriminatory features – the common external tariff, variable levies on foodstuffs and association agreements with ex-colonial possessions – which caused concern in American industrial and agricultural circles. A number of forces operated to suppress criticism of these features during the early 1960s, among them the assumed political benefits of a uniting Europe and the economic advantages conferred by access to a wider West European market. By the mid-1960s, however, the issue of EEC discrimination was unmistakably on the political agenda, partly as a result of the decline in expectations of some kind of 'Atlantic Community'. It appeared to many Americans, including some political leaders, that West European countries were receiving dynamic benefits from forms of discrimination which operated against American interests, and that the time had come for the Europeans to live up to their obligations. The feeling was reinforced by the faltering of the American economy, symptomised by the growth of the balance-of-payments deficit, domestic economic stagnation and a long-term decline in competitiveness.

From 1965 to 1970 these tensions came increasingly to head the agenda of European–American relations, alongside the issues arising from Soviet–American détente. In the trade sphere they were centred upon the attempts to reduce tariffs under the auspices of GATT – the Kennedy Round – which were dogged by the disinclination of Europeans and Americans alike to give up specific areas of protection. For the Europeans (both the EEC and Britain with its Commonwealth connections) agricultural preferences were sensitive, whereas for the Americans they were anachronistic. For the Europeans, confronted by the challenge of American multinational firms, some forms of industrial discrimination were vital, whereas for the Americans they were unjustifiable. When confronted by American claims that tariffs in Western Europe were too high, the EEC and others pointed to persistent discrimination by the United States against manufactured imports, through 'buy American' measures as well as through tariffs. Matters were complicated by the internal crisis of the EEC, partly caused by the implementation of some of the very measures in the industrial and agricultural spheres on which they were supposed to be negotiating with the United States.

At the same time the monetary pillar of the European–American economy was tottering. The commitment to a system of fixed exchange rates, with devaluations only in extreme circumstances, had done a great deal to help the growth of trade and the reconstruction of West European economies, but was incapable of rapid adjustment to match the fluctuations in economic performance which emerged in the 1960s. By 1967 the combination of American stagnation and West European dynamism (with the exception of the United Kingdom) had begun to place intolerable strains on the system, causing its members to question the benefits of participation. The French response under de Gaulle was to call for a return to the gold standard rather than a 'dollar standard' as had effectively operated up to then; while other members did not go as far as this, each had its interest in remodelling the system to suit its own needs. Most important of all, the Americans evinced considerable reluctance to continue as sole paymasters of the system. As a result the conflicting pressures on West European countries to revalue or devalue their currencies in line with their economic performances became severe, incidentally reducing the chance that some kind of European economic and monetary union would emerge.

The aggravation of these trade and monetary problems by the activities of multinational firms, who generated huge capital flows with consequent effects on currencies on both sides of the Atlantic, and the simultaneous exacerbation of American economic problems because of the Vietnam War meant that the incentive to welsh on the commitments which had been accepted (if not implemented) in the late 1940s was irresistible. A series of crises in the early 1970s effectively led to a refusal by the United States to fund the system – a repudiation of obligations by the 'banker' which effectively destroyed the regime. At the same time economic divergence in the enlarged EEC meant that the day when Western Europe could operate a zone of monetary and commercial stability was postponed indefinitely. Lip-service was still paid to the kinds of obligation which had characterised the fallen system – 'openness' rather than 'closedness', 'internationalism' rather than 'nationalism' – but they became increasingly difficult either to agree or to implement. By the mid-1970s it appeared that the postwar regime which had encapsulated the mutual obligations and commitments of West European countries and the United States was in ruins.

Quite apart from the tensions and ambiguities in the system itself, the impact of disturbance in the broader world economy was increasingly felt: the problems created by Japanese economic growth, by energy crises and by the claims of less developed countries placed an increasing strain on the remnants of the old order. Out of the ruins, however, there emerged some elements of a new order, expressing new commitments and obligations in a less precise and formal way. To a large extent the commitment on all sides was to talk – to consult and to inform about the implications of national and international trends through such mechanisms as OECD or the so-called 'Western Economic Summits', the first of which was called on French initiative in 1975. Although a commitment to consult was capable of implementation, nevertheless more specific and precise undertakings were difficult to achieve, in the face of external economic shocks and the pressures of domestic interests who demanded active defence.

Such trends had the effect of highlighting another underlying problem in the European–American economic system: the assessment and distribution of costs and benefits from its operation. Although such parallels must not be pushed too far, this question is in some respects akin to the conflicts over 'burden-sharing' in NATO. In simple language, the costs and benefits of an economic system, in the same way as those of an alliance, are likely to be unevenly distributed, with some groups being net beneficiaries and others net losers. The European–American system, with its initial stress on an 'open' trading and monetary process, was bound to leave some worse off than others. There was provision for protection of the weaker brethren, through the exchange rate activites of the IMF and the protective clauses of GATT, but it was hoped (and assumed) that recourse to these would be rare. In the end, in the early postwar years, it was also assumed that the United States would have to fund the system and bear the costs by bringing others into a condition where they could play their allotted role. After all, the American economy was dominant by virtue of its sheer size and productivity over the weakened economies of Western Europe; additionally, it depended relatively little on the process of international exchange for is continued health. Since the United States was thus relatively invulnerable to the shocks of an 'open' system, it was clearly in a position to pay quite a lot in order to get the system established. This it duly did, through the Marshall Plan and through its support of a protectionist European integration process. On the whole, during the 1950s, it was felt in the United States that the political and security benefits of a European recovery were worth paying for.

For the West Europeans the presence of an American 'banker' for the system was enormously reassuring in the period of economic recovery, shielding them from at least some of the shocks which might have attended a full-blooded implementation of the proposed economic order. A number of factors converged in the late 1950s and early 1960s to change this situation and to make the question 'who pays?' as contentious in European–American economic affairs as it became in the field of security and strategy. In fact, as already indicated at a number of points, the issues of burden-sharing in NATO and the imbalance of benefits from the Atlantic economy were interconnected, with the American balance-of-payments deficit due at least in part to military spending abroad. After the foundation of the EEC, with its common tariff wall, another major outflow of capital from the United States began, through the mechanism of investment by multinational firms who felt the need to get inside the customs union. Increasingly, the question 'who pays?' received the answer in the United States that it was the Americans who paid too much.

The perceived inequities of the changing situation made themselves felt through disputes over trade, in the context of the Kennedy Round, but the epicentre of the conflicts was unmistakably the monetary system. Although the Americans might accuse West European governments in varying degrees of failing to pay their share of the bills by adjusting their fiscal and financial policies, it was also true by the later 1960s that West Europeans suspected the Americans of having it both ways: successive United States governments did little to stem the growth of their balance-of-payments deficit, and refused to undertake domestic economic deflation in order to rectify the imbalance. It was difficult for many West Europeans to understand why they should be taken to task for failing to buy their share of American goods and services while at the same time the Americans poured billions of dollars into the Vietnam War.

Before 1971 the methods of adjustment in the Atlantic economy – the ways in which the costs were shared – were primarily internal to the countries concerned. If there was a payments deficit, then national deflationary measures were taken to reduce it: if there was a surplus, then expansionary measures could be allowed. Such a process was implicit in the idea of an open trading system with fixed exchange rates, but in August 1971, after increasing pressure on the dollar and other currencies, the Nixon government cut away much of the basis for this method of adjustment by devaluing and later floating the dollar. Henceforward, adjustments would be based on various forms of floating exchange rates which would reflect the domestic economic performance of the various countries and would almost automatically compensate for losses of competitiveness. It was extremely difficult to see any such neat rationale in the crises of 1971 and 1972, as various attempts to recreate stable exchange rates were made and abandoned, but the events of 1973 and 1974, with the generation of huge Arab oil surpluses, confirmed the demise of the old system. In some ways the 'new regime' of continuously varying exchange rates might have been seen as just another form of adjustment, replacing the internal measures demanded under the Bretton Woods system, but things were by no means as simple as that. Perhaps the greatest complicating factor was the impact of recession, which produced degrees of economic divergence unforeseen in the early 1970s and thus strained the limits of exchange rate adjustment for both the weak (the United Kingdom and, increasingly, the United States) and the strong (West Germany and the 'intruder' Japan). During the late 1970s it appeared that two additional forms of adjustment might be needed. One was 'internationalist' in form: the idea that the stronger economies could act as 'locomotives' to pull the entire Western economy out of recession. The other was 'nationalist': the idea that in a recession-hit world the onus was on national governments to secure the prosperity of their citizens, if necessary by trade restrictions or incentives. In the one version the costs of adjustment would be borne by some for the good of all; in the other, it was every country for itself, with the levers of economic management being controlled by governments responsive to domestic or parochial pressures.

The result was a crisis for the European–American economic system, which persisted into the 1980s. As much as anything else it was a crisis of scope and applicability. While it appeared that European–American economic relations were *about* more things, it also appeared that fewer of these things were subject to regulation or management by procedures agreed among the system's members. Thus, the agenda of concerns in European–American relations expanded from the 'traditional' issues of money and trade to encompass new areas of activity, many of them with important implications for economic life at regional or local levels. Despite the establishment of the International Energy Agency under the aegis of the OECD, and the European Community's efforts to create a co-ordinated energy policy among its members, it proved impossible during the 1970s and early 1980s to achieve agreement between governments on both sides of the Atlantic. Oil prices fell in real terms, and supplies eased, but this had more to do with the impact of recession than any co-ordinated effort. The same recession brought a new item to the top of the agenda: the industrial policies of West European and American governments. Although industrial policy had long been an international issue in the Atlantic arena, it became critically important in the late 1970s and early 1980s given the priority of protecting employment which was recognised by all governments. In such circumstances the promotion of exports could be – and was – seen as unfair competition leading to dumping, and the demands for protection by recession-hit industries were continual both in Western Europe and the United States. Steel, textiles, automobiles and chemicals were a focus of intense interest and of unprecedented attempts at legal regulation.

The conditions of economic interpenetration and mutual vulnerability among the countries of the Atlantic area were further complicated by external shocks and disruptions. While in the 1950s and 1960s there had been challenges to the established order – from the EEC, the Gaullists and others – these had been absorbed within a framework built upon exchange rate stability and non-discrimination, and one which contained a very large proportion of world trade. During the 1970s it became clear that the vulnerability of the system as a whole, rather than simply individual members, was acute and intensifying. One symptom of this was the increasing challenge posed by rapidly growing industrial economies outside the North Atlantic area – initially Japan, which came to dominate a number of high-technology areas, but increasingly the so-called NICs (new industrial countries) which competed fiercely in areas of heavy industry such as shipbuilding. Another symptom, dramatically highlighted in 1973 and 1974, was the extreme dependence of West European countries in particular on raw materials originating from somewhat unpredictable sources. Energy supplies especially were the focus of anxiety and concern: even the United States, which had not been heavily dependent on imported oil, was affected by the tensions of the 1970s in this respect. A final sign of vulnerability, especially for a number of West European countries, was their increasing dependence on overseas markets for maintenance of their industrial capacity: overseas trade and reliable orders became a first priority for governments, for which they were prepared to engage in considerable diplomatic activity. Linked with this trend was increasing competition in the provision of financial services such as insurance and subsidised export credits for customers.

Such indications of vulnerability for the European–American economic system were of general significance, underlining the fragility of a relatively 'open' economic area in the face of external confusion. At the same time, however, they had varying impacts on the individual members of the system. Not all countries were equally vulnerable to Japanese or NIC competition; not all were as dependent on imported oil as, say, the French or West Germans; and not all had committed themselves equally to demanding foreign customers as a sources of industrial sustenance. Thus, while some called 'wolf' at the Japanese 'invasion', others rested on 'fair trading' agreements which could be seen as forms of indirect protection. In the energy field the relatively self-sufficient British and Americans could adopt a rather less frantic tone than their more dependent brethren. Finally, in the field of trade and industry, it was noticeably easier for the United States government to call for an intensification of economic sanctions against the Soviet Union and other targets than it was for governments in West Germany and elsewhere to comply, given their distinctive patterns of trade dependence and growth.

Political Issues: Institutions, Behaviour and Values

It has become clear in the preceding discussion of strategic and economic issues that in many respects they are inseparable both from each other and from the sphere of politics and ideology. The persistence of NATO and its continuing tribulations are intimately linked to perceptions of shared values and to the exercise of power, while the postwar economic order which characterised European–American relations has always been seen as reflecting and contributing to a more explicitly political order. While it is true to say that strategy, economic affairs and 'politics' are effectively inseparable, it is also important to recognise aspects of the transatlantic relationship which are primarily located in the realm of political institutions, behaviour and values. Assumptions about the convergence both of material interests and of political ideas have been central to arguments about Atlantic 'partnership' or 'community' and demand attention in their own right, as sources of collaboration and competition.

As indicated in Chapter 3, the framework of European–American relations in the postwar period has reflected an often threatened belief in the mutual responsiveness of elites and societies, which are presented as sharing 'Western' or 'democratic' institutions and values. This has existed alongside a perceived convergence of more material interests, particularly in relation to the shape of the postwar world and the political complexion of regimes. The two factors combined – convergence of institutions and values, and material stakes in the status quo – have been seen as contributing to a natural or even an inevitable conformity of expectations and behaviour within European–American relations. On the whole, it has been assumed by participants and analysts alike that political behaviours in the Euro-American system will coincide rather than diverge. Such assumptions are much more difficult to sustain in the 1980s than in the 1950s: although it would be wrong to see the early postwar years as producing a monolithic European–American political system, the elements of pluralism and diversity have become more marked as time has passed.

In the late 1940s it was comparatively easy to discern a threat to the political institutions and values, loosely described as 'Western democratic', which formed the basis for the political systems of Western Europe. This basis was more firmly established in some societies than in others; the defeated regimes of Germany and Italy and the formerly occupied areas of northern and southern Europe had all faced severe challenges to democratic values, and in many cases faced them still through the persistence of political instability or the destruction of legitimate authority. In Germany and Italy it was assumed that major campaigns of re-education and social engineering were needed to root out the remains of fascism and Nazism; in France and the Benelux countries the destabilising impact of occupation and war created the need for new structures of authority; and in Greece particularly there was a major challenge from the activities of new adversaries, the Soviet-backed communists. These internal challenges chimed with broader uncertainties about the lines of division in the emerging postwar world to create a set of political and ideological criteria for the alignment of the United States and Western European regimes. Internally, it was necessary that legitimate regimes with 'Western' styles of operation should be restored or established, and that indigenous communist parties should be excluded from government; externally, it became clear that the developing Cold War placed a premium on compliant behaviour, which could be bolstered by the provision of military or economic assistance.

Much of the basis for this emerging political 'alliance' was of necessity intangible, based on ideas and values and on the mutual understanding of national leaderships as to the limits of acceptable behaviour. There were, however, more substantial and material factors which operated to assist the spread of 'Western' values and practices. By the very fact of their military and economic dominance, and their preponderant role in the occupation regimes in Germany and Italy, the Americans were able if not bound to influence the behaviour of local regimes. To a lesser extent this was also true of the British, who shared the occupation duties but had rather less in the way of material incentives to offer. Thus, the emergence of a federal West Germany and the reconstruction of the Italian political system in the late 1940s reflected to a large extent the priorities established by American policy-makers and shared by local Christian Democrat leaders, who were concerned not only to restore democracy, but also to prevent undesirable elements from entering government and to bolster the Atlantic Alliance. The balance of influence was by no means as clear in the case of France, where the liberation struggle and the role of the Gaullist government in exile had ensured a place for distinctively French priorities. In the case of Britain, where intimate wartime collaboration and a shared appreciation of the political situation on the whole sustained a 'special relationship', conformity was seen as almost automatic and instinctive whatever disagreements might arise on specific issues.

By the early 1950s, therefore, it could be argued that a political 'alliance' akin to those in the strategic and economic spheres was in the making. As in these other spheres, the United States held the initiative in the consolidation of the 'alliance': it was American policy-makers who pronounced the doctrines and defined the threats which were to form the rationale for collaboration. Through their confrontation with Soviet policies and the growing competition for the allegiance of uncommitted areas, successive United States governments also set the broader pattern of the postwar status quo, in relation to which conformity and deviation could be judged. The lines were in many respects quite tightly drawn, especially in terms of the role to be played by domestic communist parties and in terms of contacts with the regimes of the Soviet bloc. Yet there were a series of inherent tensions in the kind of political and ideological alignment which emerged, and these have persisted in one form or another until the present day. It was assumed that there would be a consensus – and thus a good deal of conformity – in approaches to the postwar settlement, both in West European politics and in the international arena, but in fact there was considerable underlying diversity in the aims of West European regimes and in their interpretation of the status quo. American policy-makers and those in Western Europe assumed that American strategic and economic dominance would enhance Washington's ability to secure compliance from its West European allies, but in the political and diplomatic field resources were not always so tangible and easily identifiable. In the same way the unifying effects either of an outside political threat or of doctrinal initiatives were likely to be more subject to redefinition and differences of view than was the case in the strategic or economic fields. Thus, the extent of political conformity and deviation as between the United States and West European countries has been a major source of debate and tensions almost since the beginning of the postwar era.

As has already been noted, the major political commitments undertaken by West European governments, and sustained by successive American leaderships, were two: first, a commitment to the emerging division of Europe between the Soviet and American spheres of influence, and thus to the division of Germany; and secondly, a commitment to a balance of forces within West European societies which focused on the development of more or less capitalist and democratic parties. These commitments were often left unstated and implicit, but there were more formal expressions, for example, in the Truman Doctrine and in the North Atlantic Treaty itself. In addition, the assumptions and pronouncements of American policy-makers such as Dulles not only took these commitments as almost axiomatic, but also saw them as leading to a distinct – and subordinate – role for Western Europe in the international system. On the whole, the acquiescence of the regimes concerned was achieved – most effectively in the case of West Germany and Italy, less surely in the case of France. But even where the compliance of political leaderships and elites was achieved, it was never entirely sure that their images of a desirable international system would coincide with that of the United States.

During the 1950s, therefore, it appeared that the dilution of either a West European or American commitment to the postwar political order would be a reflection of differing views about the developing international system, rather than of the erosion of domestic consensus or authority. The key would lie in the status and assumed roles of the countries engaged, which often fluctuated or diverged markedly. West Germany, which under the leadership of Adenauer had single-mindedly pursued rehabilitation within the context of the Western Alliance and the European Community, was none the less a source of some uncertainty, given the residual neutralism of the Social Democratic Party and the influence of Soviet appeals for a comprehensive Central European settlement. On the whole, however, West Germany's position was by the late 1950s less insecure or fluctuating than that of the French, who had steadily built up a tradition of deviant behaviour with respect to the Cold War and its lines of battle, and whose leadership was increasingly affected by domestic instabilities. Although the British were committed to a view of East–West relations which largely coincided with that of American policy-makers, the persistence of global responsibilities and assumptions of a world role as intermediaries made them a less than wholly predictable force.

Meanwhile, on the American side, the responsibility of political leadership and bargaining authority in East–West dealings had been almost eagerly undertaken in the early 1950s, but the beginnings of realistic negotiations with the Soviet Union in the final years of the Eisenhower administration had had a corrosive effect on the confidence felt by West European governments. The period 1957–60, in fact, demonstrated in embryo some of the features which were to be highlighted by the Nixon–Kissinger détente policies of 1968–74: a temptation for the United States to bargain directly with the Soviet Union, the threatened marginalisation of European interests and initiatives, and thus a decline in consensus within European–American relations on the future of the political order. Thus, while British governments especially attempted to mediate or to plan for disengagement in Central Europe, with interest from both France and West Germany, the Americans often seemed to assume a lofty lack of interest.

The consolidation of European–American consensus on a view of postwar political order took a step further in 1957–58 with the coming into force of the Treaty of Rome and the establishment of the EEC – an organisation explicitly based on requirements of democratic rule in member-states. Paradoxically, though, and to the frustration of the Kennedy administration and its successors, the political implications of the EEC seemed to diverge from the expectations of 'Atlanticists'. The policies of Gaullist France seemed designed to use European economic integration as a vehicle for influence and as the basis for a European concert or coalition, rather than a 'partner' for American interests. In fact, Gaullism took as one of its major tenets a lack of commitment to rigid lines of political demarcation in Europe or in the wider world, relying upon a reassertion of sovereignty and autonomy which were seen as threatened by American policies. By doing so the French policies of the early 1960s established one of the major motifs of events in the later part of the decade, and a major source of tensions in the political field. While these tensions had been muted in the 1950s by the needs of economic reconstruction and strategic consolidation, it became clear that there were important differences of view within Western Europe, and between West European countries and the United States, on the shape and permanence of the 'Cold War coalitions'.

Central to this emerging set of tensions was the question of Germany. Twenty years after the end of the Second World War there was still no settlement which gave an agreed shape or status to Germany, and the consolidation of rival regimes in the GDR and GFR had left open the possibility of reunification as a matter of principle if not of practical policy. The Gaullist 'deviation' of the early and mid-1960s had in fact been based partly on an attempt to construct a French–West German coalition, but the issues of the later 1960s depended less on this than on the reassertion of some specifically German interests through the pursuit of *Ostpolitik*. For European–American relations the issue was crucial, since at the same time the development of American–Soviet détente raised the possibility of a redefinition of the European status quo in a global context. It was at this point that the previously secure – though not unchallenged – consensus on political forms in Europe came under a pressure from which it did not recover during the 1970s and early 1980s. The process of détente at the superpower level could not be relied upon to safeguard the interest of West Europeans or to recognise the nuances of the European political order. On the other hand, American assumptions that West Europeans would honour their obligations by following where the superpowers led could no longer be unquestioned. Economic and strategic recovery in Western Europe (and especially in West Germany) had gone hand in hand with a political recovery and a resurgence of self-confidence which could not be held in check.

The course of détente and *Ostpolitik* in the period 1970–4 thus became intertwined and often delicately balanced, and a good deal of effort was needed on both sides to preserve the kind of consultation and broad agreement which would not jeopardise both. Perhaps the most telling conclusion drawn by many from the episode was in terms of the respective European and American commitments to an easing of tensions in Europe. Whereas the United States could see European détente as a means to an end, and a potentially reversible process, the needs of the Germans especially dictated an altogether more wholehearted view of the phenomenon as an end in itself. The growth of a specifically West European view was assisted by the development of political co-operation in the EEC, and reflected a growing economic and social intermingling of West and East European societies. It implied a rejection of the assumption that 'America knows best' which was embodied in pronouncements such as Henry Kissinger's 'Year of Europe' speech in 1973, and although it was confined in the first place to the problem of Central Europe, it formed a basis for later extensions into other areas of conflict or tension.

The middle and late 1970s were littered with signs that the balance of political initiative as between the United States and Western Europe had shifted. In the Conference on Security and Co-operation in Europe (CSCE), which produced the 1975 Helsinki Declaration, the EEC countries operated a co-ordinated policy, and they later made known their disapproval of some of the Carter administration's wilder pronouncements on human rights in Eastern Europe. The Middle East saw attempts at major West European initiatives, to the annoyance of American policy-makers who were anxious to preserve the Camp David process. Most dramatically, the attempts of the Reagan administration to declare a 'new Cold War' in the early 1980s met with a response in Western Europe which stressed the need for continuing dialogue and détente and which was profoundly unsettling for American policy-makers.

Quite apart from these tensions over the political shape and future of Europe, the 1970s especially gave evidence that domestic political changes in Western Europe and the United States themselves could create conflicts, eroding the confidence and consensus on which much of the postwar order depended. This was by no means a new trend – as already noted, attention to the internal compliance of West European regimes was a building-block of the Euro-American political system – but in the 1970s it was exacerbated by the loss of domestic political legitimacy which occurred on both sides of the Atlantic. Two major symptoms of the malaise became evident in the years after 'Watergate' and the energy crisis: first, political leaders found that they were forced to pay attention to a number of new issues by the pressure exerted by domestic interests; a new political introspection and new 'nationalism' emerged to parallel that in the economic sphere. At the same time, the frailties of domestic leaderships were suspected of having effects on their international reliability, either because of the assumed influence of 'Eurocommunism' or 'Eurosocialism', or because of simple unpredictability and erratic behaviour. The political homogeneity of the Euro-American system, and thus the consensus around which much of its strategic and economic apparatus had been built, was open to challenge, and it was no longer clear what the extent of commitment to a given vision of political order or values could be.

It was argued earlier that in the spheres of strategy and economic affairs divergence of perceptions as to obligations and commitments were reflected in more limited tensions over 'burden-sharing'. In European–American relations 'who pays?' has always been a burning question, and in defence programmes or economic exchanges there are some very material costs to weigh in the balance. The question in the political sphere is not so easy to answer, and the factors involved are less easy to quantify, but it is none the less an important aspect of the relationship. The burdens to be assessed are defined in terms of diplomatic activity and doctrinal initiatives, and in terms of a basic tension between the costs and benefits of conformity. Thus, in the early stages of the postwar relationship it was undoubtedly the Americans who bore the burden of cementing transatlantic links and of defending Western Europe through diplomacy and bargaining. Such a situation was largely in line with the economic and strategic demands of the Western Alliance, and depended on American willingness to bear the burden. But things were not quite as simple as that: the postwar 'bargain' also demanded that West European countries should pay through the loss of autonomy in broadly political areas. In a sense, therefore, the bargain was mutual, with both sides offering resources and bearing costs in order to promote solidarity. Not all West European parties to the bargain gave up equal measures of autonomy – the British retained an independent role in many areas, and the French reasserted theirs during the 1950s – but on the whole during the Cold War years there was a readiness on both sides to bear this burden, in the cause of overriding political and doctrinal needs.

It was in the 1960s that the 'burden-sharing' arrangements in the political field began to experience strains not dissimilar from those which had emerged in strategic and economic affairs. The political recovery of Europe created in many quarters a desire to retake the political initiative, and to wrest from the United States some of the political and ideological privileges which successive administrations had come to expect. Gaullism, and later the West German assertion of their interests in *Ostpolitik*, were the chief expressions of this new feeling, but it was also expressed for many West Europeans in the hope of a co-ordinated foreign policy for the EEC members. The process, however, came up against a number of barriers. In the first place, there were bound to be tensions if a willingness to act as equal with the Americans in the political and diplomatic spheres was not matched by a similar willingness to share the (more material) burden of strategic and economic responsibility. Secondly, it was clear that West European inclinations to expand their political role and 'presence' were mainly limited to the affairs of Europe itself, and did not encompass the broader problems of the international system. Additionally, although the EEC could provide a framework for a good deal of policy co-ordination at the declaratory level, it appeared that none of its major members wanted it to become anything more than a 'civil power', without the kind of unity in the security field which would add muscle to its diplomacy.

The limitations of West European concerns and activities in the political sphere were compounded by a distinct reluctance on the part of American policy-makers to share the burden of leadership. Although during the 1950s the British had been able to carve out a niche for themselves in summit diplomacy, this came to an end in the early 1960s and was not taken up by the emerging forces of France or West Germany despite their sometimes vociferous demands. Given that there were real doctrinal and diplomatic differences between the United States and major West European countries throughout the 1960s and into the 1970s, this lack of a substantial West European contribution was bound to cause tensions. After rumbling for much of the later 1960s, the real climax of the growing contradictions came in 1973, with the call by Henry Kissinger for a redefinition of the political 'rules' for transatlantic relations. Kissinger's expressed hope that West European countries might begin to take their share of the responsibility for the global order was hedged around with qualifications, and came to mean even less in the light of American unilateralism during the crisis of October 1973. The Americans seemed unwilling to relinquish anything more than a token amount of responsibility, yet at the same time appeared to demand their traditional privileges. This impression was borne out by the events of the late 1970s and 1980s; the Americans demanded diplomatic support and often material sacrifice against Iran, the Soviet Union and others, but were reluctant to recognise the specific interests and responsibilities of West European governments. In 1982 the tensions over the American demand for sanctions against the Soviet Union led Vice-President Bush to declare that the United States was the leader of the free world and intended to act the part. Whereas in 1950 such a statement might have appeared routine, by 1982 it amounted almost to open provocation.

The limits of political conformity have thus been challenged increasingly within the Euro-American system as the political reconstruction of West European countries has first been achieved and then consolidated, and as American confidence has fluctuated. From a position in the early 1950s when commitment to the European status quo was generally high, and the allocation of diplomatic and doctrinal responsibilities was based on a high level of consensus, a steady increase in diversity and tensions can be charted. As a result, the boundaries of the political 'alliance' in European–American relations have been constantly open to challenge and redefinition. Successive United States administrations have assumed that their presence in Western Europe and their stated commitment to its defence have given them the right to pronounce upon the appropriate political shape of the continent. While this was to all intents and purposes true in the Cold War years, it cannot be taken for granted in periods of less obvious confrontation or international tension. This is especially the case when regimes in Western Europe are faced – as they were increasingly during the 1970s – with the need to satisfy domestic demands of a pressing and sometimes radical nature. In parallel fashion, the linking of diplomatic conformity under American leadership with domestic political conformity appeared during the early Cold War years to be an almost inevitable state of affairs. As political reconstruction bred political confidence and assertiveness, the American assumption that their judgements on domestic political performance would be heeded could no longer fully be justified. Far from proving a buttress for continued compliance in Western Europe, the EEC often proved to be a channel for the expression of dissent and non-conformity.

A marked growth of pluralism is thus the dominant trend in the political relations between the United States and Western Europe. As in the economic and strategic spheres, there has been a shifting of the balance between the various parties to the arrangements made or assumed in the aftermath of the Second World War, and a growing willingness in Western Europe to assert the diversity of interests and objectives. Although this tendency is highlighted by crises and increases in levels of international tension (as in the period 1980–2), it is not created by such conditions alone. There seem to be four central factors which contribute to the growth and to the recognition of diversity in the Euro-American system, in fact. The first is the extent and the confidence of American assertiveness, which in the 1980s has been greater in the field of political dogma than in the areas of strategy or economic affairs. The second is the level of global tension – mainly influenced by American–Soviet relations – which has swung from Cold War to détente and then some way back towards the former. This is associated with a third: the level of perceived pluralism in Eastern Europe, and the extent to which West European societies or governments respond to it. Finally, the relative salience of domestic needs (whether political or economic) as opposed to international or alliance needs clearly plays a role in influencing the desire to conform to some kind of transatlantic orthodoxy. In the early 1980s American assertiveness has been erratic and contested, global tensions have fluctuated, Eastern Europe has been in a state of flux and domestic preoccupations have been at the head of most agendas. Diversity, pluralism, confusion even, have thus never been far from the European–American scene, placing great pressure on the processes of management and co-ordination which have developed over the period since 1945.

Further Reading

The very nature of a focus on 'issues' makes practically everything that has ever been written about European–American relations potentially relevant. However, the ideas which are central to this chapter can be found in explicit form in the following selections. For general treatments which refer in a sustained way to the strategic, economic and political dimensions of transatlantic relations, see especially: Alting von Geusau (1983); Hahn and Pfaltzgraff (1979); Hanrieder (1974); Kaiser and Schwartz (1977); Pfaltzgraff (1969); Trezise (1975); and Wilcox and Haviland (1963).

On specific areas, the following are useful.

Strategic issues: On alliance (and NATO) in general, see: Buchan (1960); Fedder (1973); Fox and Fox (1967); Freedman (1981–2); Hoffmann (1979); Kissinger (1957, 1960, 1965); Osgood (1962, 1968); Tucker and Wrigley (1983); and Williams (1977). On perceptions of threat and commitment, see: Fox and Schilling (1973); Furniss (1956, 1961); Harrison (1981); Knorr (1959); Pierre (1973); Treverton (1980); and Williams (1982). Nuclear strategy and debates are covered in: Hoag (1958); Mandelbaum (1979); Patterson and Furniss (1957); Ranger (1981); Treverton (1979); Wohlstetter (1961); and Wolfers (1958). The problem of 'burden-sharing' is explored in various ways in: Calleo (1970); Gordon (1956b); Kolodziej (1980–1); Lunn (1983); Newhouse (1971); and Stanley (1965). Finally, the problem of NATO's area of operation (geographical and functional) is covered in: Artner (1980); Coker (1982); Garfinkle (1981); Miller (1974); Spiegel (1982); and Woolcock (1982).

Economic issues: The changing character of the European–American economic regime is covered in: Shonfield *et al.* (1976); and Spero (1981). Both of these pay particular attention to the assumptions and 'rules' of the Western system. The more specifically 'Atlantic' characteristics receive attention in: Calleo and Rowland (1973); Cooper (1968); Hanrieder (1982); Hinshaw (1964); and Krause (1969). The emergence of the EEC and the problem of adjustment are dealt with in: van der Beugel (1966); Camps (1967); Diebold (1960); Wallich (1968); and Warnecke (1972). Calleo (1982) is a critical treatment of American policies in general. More specific policy disputes are the subject of countless treatments. On trade, the following are a sample: Benoit (1961); Casadio (1973); Cooper (1972–3); Krause (1968); Preeg (1970); and Woolcock (1982). The area of industrial policy is well covered in Diebold (1980). Financial and monetary issues are explored in: Bergsten (1981); King (1982); Krause and Salant (1973); Trezise (1979); and Triffin (1978–9). The energy problem can be pursued in: Kaiser (1978); Lieber (1974, 1980); *Orbis* (1980); and Vernon (1976).

Political issues: On some important stages in the developing political 'balance' between the United States and Western Europe, see: Cromwell (1978); Kaiser (1973, 1974); Serfaty (1979); and Tucker (1981). The 'Atlantic system' is dealt with in: Buchan (1962–3); Calleo (1965); Cleveland (1966); Cromwell *et al.* (1969); and Kaiser (1966–7). Disputes over the form of Europe are covered more or less explicitly in: Brzezinski (1965); DePorte (1979); Joffe (1983); and Morgan (1974). Problems connected with the internal workings of societies can be pursued in: Duroselle (1977); Grosser (1980); Landes (1977); Webb (1979), and Zoppo (1980).

5 Processes: the Conduct of European–American Relations

Chapters 3 and 4 examined two elements of the 'Euro-American system' – the environment within which it exists, and the issues on which it has centred. The conclusion has been in general that European–American relations are carried on in a complex, multifaceted and often indeterminate environment, and that they are centred on a multiplicity of issues which often overlap and coexist rather uneasily. Implicit in the discussion, however, has been a third element of the system: the techniques, methods and channels through which the relationships are sustained or pursued. Much of the literature in the broad field of international relations focuses on the ways in which the actors within the international system relate to and communicate with each other, and clearly any study of European–American relations would be incomplete without such a treatment of communication and mutual influence.

The focus of this chapter is therefore on the conduct of relations between the United States and the countries of Western Europe, with the aim of identifying the major elements in the network of communications to which they give rise. As noted in Chapter 2, it is possible to conceive of these communications as naturally harmonious, and to discern some kind of almost instinctive convergence between the policies and actions of governments on both sides of the Atlantic, giving rise to a 'community' of interests and fates. The argument in Chapters 3 and 4 should alert the reader to a rather more complex and less comfortable reality. In European–American relations a variety of actors – governmental and non-governmental – coexist, pursuing their policies at a variety of levels and through a number of possible channels. Quite naturally, in such a diverse system, lines of communication are not always clear; equally, the 'messages' sent out by one participant may not be received or understood clearly by those for whom they are intended. The ground-rules of interpretation or criticism may not be as precise or uncontested as they should, despite (or perhaps because of) the proliferation of elaborate institutional and organisational frameworks. Above all, the expression of intentions or objectives and the achievement

of co-ordinated action to influence the course of events in the real world
may be subject to many kinds of national and other obstacles.

In the final analysis, then, this chapter is about the exercise of
influence, whether by governments or various other subnational and
international bodies. That the influence can be collaborative or
conflictual, constructive or destructive, is clear; the aim here is to clarify
the components of the problem as they affect European–American
relations. Four patterns of communication are dealt with: first, the
exercise of hegemonic power by the United States and its erosion;
secondly, the cultivation of 'special' or 'privileged' relationships; thirdly,
the attempt at policy co-ordination within Western Europe; and finally,
the growth of institutions aimed at the management of interdependence
in the Atlantic area.

The USA: from Hegemony to Uncertainty

Although it can be argued that the process of American entanglement
in the affairs of Western Europe was by no means inevitable or clear-
cut, there is little doubt that once the United States became committed
to a role in transatlantic relations the role was that of a dominant power.
Given the resources in both the military and the economic field on which
the United States government could call, such a development was hardly
surprising – in fact, the policies of several West European leaderships
(the British and West Germans most notably) were based on the
overriding need to secure as many of those resources as possible for the
military security and economic reconstruction of Western Europe. The
presence of 300,000 American troops in NATO member-countries, and
the disbursement of an estimated $19 billion through the agency of the
Marshall Plan and the European Recovery Programme, were the fruits
of this concerted effort to shelter under the American wing.

The reality of American dominance could thus be felt in a variety of
forms during the 1950s and into the 1960s; in the immediate postwar
years and during the height of the Cold War the influence was largely
exercised on a governmental level, but there was a shift in the late 1950s
and the 1960s. The private 'invasion' of Western Europe by American-
based multinational corporations and financial institutions added a new
dimension to American preponderance, to the alarm of some West
European observers; none the less, it was often closely associated with
United States government policies and expressed in another tangible
form the continuing weight of the United States in the transatlantic
balance.

It was not only in the sphere of activities and enterprises that American
hegemony could be discerned, however. As noted in Chapter 4, many
of the institutions of the postwar economic and strategic order in the

Western world were marked by a structural dominance on the part of the Americans. Again, there was a certain inevitability about this: in NATO it initially appeared that only the British were capable of making even a minor material contribution, and the American 'majority shareholding' in the Alliance commands was simply a reflection of their strategic role. In the economic sphere the position was less clear-cut, since the Truman administration and its successors encouraged a positive European role in the framing of institutions for economic recovery and integration; but it must be remembered that the European initiatives were hedged around with American provisos and emerged against a broader background of the Bretton Woods financial system and GATT trading systems, which broadly reflected American preferences.

The 'American preferences' against which European–American relations were frequently judged during the 1950s and 1960s can be seen as constituting a quasi-ideology of 'Atlanticism' and liberalism. Indeed, some writers have gone so far as to discern in American attitudes to the Western economic and strategic systems the ideological basis for a form of empire, within which the West Europeans were assigned a subordinate place and expected to adhere to a number of more or less formal requirements. In the strategic sphere the Atlantic Alliance expressed the predominance of American strategic thinking as well as American aims; in the economic sphere the drive towards an 'open' world economy based on fixed exchange rates with the dollar as a medium of exchange 'as good as gold', and the abhorrence of discriminatory trading practices, provided the other foundation of hegemony. Between 1945 and 1955 it could also be argued that the consolidation of ideologically conforming regimes in a number of West-European countries set the seal on an essentially 'imperial' system.

Whether or not it is belived that there was a conscious American drive to establish an 'Atlantic empire', it is clear that the position of American postwar predominance and its progressive modification during the 1960s and the 1970s have had important implications for the conduct of European–American relations. It was seen in Chapters 3 and 4 that during the early Cold War years much attention had to be paid on both sides of the Atlantic to domestic political processes in the United States. By the nature of American predominance, it was likely that the vagaries of congressional competition and the ability of 'Atlanticists' to promote the cause of Western Europe on Capitol Hill and in the White House would be a determining influence in the Western Alliance. Both the Marshall Plan and its succeeding programmes of economic assistance, and NATO with its material military commitments, had to be 'sold' to a number of domestic constituencies in the United States, which meant they were constantly open to fluctuations in the American political climate. While it was never likely that either set of commitments would be overturned, it was always possible that far-reaching decisions could be taken by American administrations for essentially parochial reasons.

At the same time as American predominance dictated a major role for domestic pressures in American attitudes towards Western Europe, it gave rise to a particular style of behaviour in transatlantic politics. This pattern of action could be termed 'hegemonic intervention', but in a way that is too positive a conception. The fact is that in the 1950s, whether by accident or design, the Americans on several occasions succeeded in shaping European–American relations by action taken on a largely unilateral basis. Thus, Dulles was able to threaten an 'agonizing reappraisal' of American commitments at the height of the EDC controversy; the operations of the OEEC in implementing the European Recovery Programme were subject to redefinition and 'guidance' from a variety of American sources; and the status of communist parties in Western Europe was subject to consistent scrutiny by anxious American leaders.

During the 1950s the pattern largely continued. It was most marked in the sphere of nuclear weapons and strategy, where the development of Soviet capabilities and the availability of new generations of tactical weapons created a series of pressures and incentives for American policy-makers. These factors made themselves felt in Western Europe through the American insistence that new types of weapons must be stationed there, although the implications of a war fought with nuclear (or for that matter, chemical) weapons on West European soil were a source of much agonising by allied governments. Meanwhile, suspicions were increasing in the United States itself that a number of West European allies were reluctant to boost their conventional forces to agreed levels at the expense of economic reconstruction, and there was the beginning of the veiled threat to withdraw American forces if the conventional burden was not met – a threat which surfaced explicitly in Congress during the late 1960s and early 1980s.

The exercise of American muscle in the economic field was more discreet, at least until the full impact of the EEC was felt during the 1960s. Rather than 'hegemonic intervention', American policy during the genesis of the EEC could better be described as 'hegemonic abstention', allowing the implications of earlier economic decisions to feed through into a new phase of integration despite the potential costs. Two qualifications can be noted here: first, the Americans took an active role in discouraging British attempts to dilute the integration process; and secondly, they were active in boosting the European Atomic Energy Community (Euratom) through financial aid while taking care that it could not be extended into any military applications.

While the 1950s had seen the high point of American dominance in material terms – a dominance which was beginning to wane by the end of the decade – it was in the 1960s that the most overt attempt to impose a Washington-inspired framework on European–American relations emerged. Beyond doubt, President Kennedy's call for an 'Atlantic partnership' between the United States and a uniting Europe expressed the 'ideological initiative' which was assumed to lie with a dominant power; but, as noted in Chapter 1, it was unleashed at a time when the growing national assertiveness of many West European societies made them less willing to accept it. In truth, the 'grand design' as a model for the conduct of European–American relations was not based on an even-handed partnership; never was it suggested (at least in Washington) that American predominance in the strategic field would be relinquished, and in many ways the exercise constituted an attempt to reimpose 'Atlanticism' on a Western Europe which was seen as potentially deviating from the path of righteousness, in both the military and the economic spheres.

It is evident with hindsight that the proclamation of the 'grand design' ushered in a period of transition in the conduct of European–American relations rather than the reaffirmation of American predominance. The attempt to reassert American strategic dominance within NATO was met by French recalcitrance and withdrawal from the integrated command, while the multilateral force proposal, which had a strongly 'Atlanticist' tinge to its plans for a multinational naval nuclear force using essentially American weapons systems, was ditched in recognition of the reservations held by both nuclear (the United Kingdom) and non-nuclear (West Germany especially) allies. In the economic sphere it became clear that for a variety of reasons the EEC members were unwilling or unable to subscribe in full to 'Atlanticist' ideals, and also that the negotiation of trade reforms was less a matter of American predominance than even-handed or cut-throat bargaining. West European governments could also increasingly point to the 'irresponsibility' of Washington's economic management as the balance of-payments deficit grew and the dollar came under pressure, and they were able to raise the embarrassing question of Vietnam in any discussion of the right or duty of the United States to lead the 'free world'.

By the end of the 1960s the exercise of American influence in European–American relations was unpredictable, to say the least. At one level – that of negotiations with the Soviet Union for a relaxation of tensions – the Americans still seemed to lead from the front, although the West Germans caused complications over *Ostpolitik* and there were constant murmurings about the need for consultation from other allies. Also, in the NATO context, remnants of a hegemonic role could be discerned, although the apparatus of consultation with the allies was extended as a result of the 1960s crisis. Economically, the picture was far more blurred: although the American economy and the dollar were still potent forces, the commitment of United States governments to any set of rules – 'Atlanticist' or other – for the management of the world economy was difficult to estimate. Politically, the American mood of introspection and withdrawal as Vietnam approached its climax was one which did not lend itself to a reassertion of leadership and commitments.

During the 1970s and 1980s these features of America's role have formed a central enigma in the conduct of Atlantic relations. In the United States itself the impact of 'Watergate' and economic recession created a profound mood of introspection and self-interest (partly paralleled in Western Europe) and a loss of legitimacy in some of the institutions and elites which had underpinned 'Atlanticism'. In American foreign policy more generally, the impact of Vietnam and of domestic fragmentation have been seen as responsible for a lack of consistency and a failure to generate appropriate strategies for a rapidly changing international situation. It is not that American leaders have been unable or unwilling to pronounce on world events and to formulate doctrines: the 'Nixon Doctrine', the 'Carter Doctrine' and the powerful but as of 1983 unchristened 'Reagan Doctrine' have all made their mark, but it has become evident that they are backed at best by a fragmented and erratic form of hegemony.

In European–American relations the consequences of this trend have been felt especially in the fluctuations of American international behaviour. In matters both economic and military American policy is still able to create profound effects on the societies of Western Europe but the policy itself has become unpredictable and often contradictory. There are, however, a number of relatively familiar elements in the conduct of Washington's policies towards the European allies. First, there is the element of 'linkage' – the attempt to use demands or concessions in one field as an incentive to agreements in others. This is a longstanding theme in American policy towards Western Europe – think of the Marshall Plan and NATO, for example – but only in the 1970s and 1980s has it become an explicit and consistent demand. Very often it occurs in respect of another venerable issue, that of European contributions to the conventional strength of NATO, but it has also been used to further American demands on more general anti-Soviet measures such as economic sanctions. In one way the practice of 'linkage' can be seen as a response to the erosion of American hegemony; a truly hegemonial power would not need to indulge in such a tactic so openly or so frequently (and with such limited success). But another feature of recent American policy towards Western Europe represents more of a refusal to recognise decline than a response to it; despite calls for a responsible 'devolution of power' to the West European allies which have been repeated at frequent intervals since the mid-1960s, there has been no explicit or concerted attempt by any American administration to resolve some of the structural problems in the Western Alliance.

The impact of changes in the United States role on the conduct of

European–American relations has thus been patchy and difficult to pin down. At the level of declaratory policy, assertions of leadership and the commitment of the United States to Western Europe have continued, but the policy in operation has often seemed formless and capricious. Much of the apparatus of American hegemony is still in place, but it operates in a rather creaky manner if at all. On both sides of the Atlantic the influence of domestic and parochial pressures seems to have eroded the responsiveness which enabled American leaders to 'sell' the leadership of the Western Alliance and European leaders to justify their acceptance of the American presence. The 'transmission belts' of American influence on the affairs of Western Europe are not in good repair it seems, and the history of the early 1980s confirms this impression. While the Americans demanded West European acquiescence in changes of nuclear weaponry, there was often a distinct lack of certainty about the United States posture on defence and disarmament; at the same time European criticism of American refusal to bear the economic burdens of reflation came up against the Reagan administration's reluctance to reduce interest rates. All in all, the situation in 1982–3 encapsulated many of the trends of the preceding decade, in more or less dramatic form.

This last assessment indicates something which is rather muted in a treatment centred on American dominance and its decline: the role of the West European countries, individually or collectively, which is the 'other side of the coin'. In the next two sections the discussion focuses on two aspects of European responses to American influence: first, the phenomenon of 'special relationships'; and secondly, the idea of a European 'caucus' or voice in transatlantic dealings.

'Special Relationships' and Strained Relationships

It is in many ways natural to assume that a dominant power such as the United States will seek to exercise its dominance at least in part through the creation of 'special' or 'privileged' relationships with some of those who fall within its sphere of influence. In the same way it is to be expected that some of the subordinate powers will seek to cultivate intimate ties with their protector. While it could be argued that this trend is the equivalent of an imperial 'divide and rule' strategy, it seems that in European–American relationships a considerable role is also played by the complexity of the environment and of the interests engaged (see Chapter 3). The relationship of each West European society with the United States has been somewhat special; in this section there is an attempt to point out some of the varieties which have emerged, and some of the changes which have affected them.

Perhaps the best-known 'special relationship' in transatlantic relations – and until recently the most studied – has been that of the

'Anglo-Saxons', Britain and the United States. During the Second World War there had been extremely close collaboration at the political, military and economic levels between leaders and officials of the two powers, and it was assumed by many that this would continue into the postwar period. Such an assumption overlooked a number of areas of open contention between British and American policies, of which three in particular were relevant to the broader sweep of European–American relations. First, the British had assumed that they would retain a kind of strategic parity with the Americans, extending even into the nuclear field; it became quite rapidly and painfully clear that this was not to be, although close collaboration did emerge, and the 1950s witnessed a gradual British adjustment to a form of nuclear dependency which reflected their lack of options and resources. Secondly, the British found themselves at odds with American policy in the area of decolonisation (as also did the French, of which more shortly). Part of the American design for a liberal world order demanded the dismantling of colonial empires and of the economic discrimination they often entailed. Although the British withdrawal from their colonial obligations was rapid and relatively painless during the 1950s and early 1960s, there were still frictions with successive American administrations, and the 'neo-colonial' episode at Suez brought many of them to renewed life. Finally, the British were reluctant to accept the logic of American policy on the postwar economic order, and especially the emergence of an integrated Western Europe, which clashed with their preferences for Commonwealth economic organisation. The tensions between British and American policies towards the EEC during the late 1950s have already been noted, but these reflected a longstanding set of contradictions which had (for example) seen the British, as major recipients of Marshall Aid, stand out against the implied pressure to join a uniting Europe in the early 1950s.

It has been said more than once that by the late 1950s the Anglo-American 'special relationship' was special only for the British, as a source of consolation in hard times. The events of December 1962 and January 1963 proved that this was not entirely true; de Gaulle's veto of British entry into the EEC (which had been a major implicit part of Kennedy's 'grand design') reflected his view that the United Kingdom would be an agent or 'Trojan horse' for American dominance in the EEC much as it appeared to be in NATO. The impression seems to have been confirmed by the Nassau Agreement of December 1962 which entailed the supply of Polaris missiles to Britain. These two months were in many ways the high point of the British–American relationship, although no one would see the effects as entirely helpful for any country concerned. From the mid-1960s onwards, and especially after British entry into the EEC in January 1973, the links between the 'Anglo-Saxon' powers came more and more to resemble the relations between the

United States and other Atlantic nations, with two major exceptions. Whereas in the early 1960s the Americans had been reluctant to further British ambitions in the nuclear field, in the late 1970s they proved more willing to provide London with a successor to Polaris (the Trident system). The effects of this decision – combined with the acceptance of large numbers of American-controlled Cruise missiles by the Conservative government – were ambiguous, restoring British credentials as a 'loyal ally' but creating major political controversy in Britain itself. At the same time, the links between the American and British 'intelligence communities' continued to be intimate. In 1948 secret agreements had established arrangements for a 'division of labour' in the monitoring of world events, which continued to operate in the 1980s. Such arrangements were seen to be in the interests of both parties – and proved useful to the British especially during the Falklands conflict of 1982.

If Britain might be seen as the American 'agent' in Western Europe for certain purposes (a title disputed with the West Germans, as will be seen later), no such label could be attached to France. Under both the 4th and 5th Republics the French have aptly been described as 'reluctant allies', determined to reassert national autonomy and in the process to throw off many of the shackles imposed by American dominance. The postwar links between the United States and France were rather different from those between London and Washington; during the war de Gaulle as leader of the Free French had constantly fought against the arrogance and lack of consideration which he attributed to the Anglo-Saxons, and the postwar dependence of France in the strategic and economic spheres only served to strengthen these feelings in its population and its leadership. As already noted, in NATO the French were accorded only token rank as one of the leading members, and 4th Republic leaders constantly fought to rectify this perceived injustice. In economic matters, although the French were at the centre of European integration, they remained reluctant to subject their national planning processes to influence from the United States. Politically, the search for a re-establishment of French prestige and autonomy produced a strong resistance to any dilution of sovereignty except where this could not be avoided.

The results of this set of tensions were felt increasingly as the 1950s progressed. As noted in Chapter 1, the French were at the centre of the crisis over the failure of the European Defence Community, first imposing conditions on the extent to which they would contribute to a 'European army' and then proving unable to muster a majority for ratification even after all the concessions had been attached. In common with the British, the French felt the pressure of American anti-colonialism, but in their case the road to decolonisation was a traumatic one, marked by wars in Indochina and North Africa, and by the eventual fall of the 4th Republic in the face of the Algerian crisis. In the field of European integration, French willingness to proceed was conditioned by the benefits which would accrue especially to agricultural interests, and the resulting Common Agricultural Policy of the EEC was to become a major cause of contention with the United States between the 1960s and 1980s.

Crisis point in Franco-American relations was reached in the early 1960s, with de Gaulle's reassertion of French autonomy and his demand for equal consideration with Britain and the United States in NATO. The effects of this confrontation – between 'Grand Design' and 'Grand Ambition' as Grosser puts it – are set out at other points in this book, and culminated in the French withdrawal from the NATO integrated command during 1966. In addition, de Gaulle made significant efforts, in pursuit of his idea of a 'Europe des patries', to entice the West Germans into a closer entente with France, and to hold back important steps on the road to European economic integration. The final years of de Gaulle's regime saw perhaps the most bitter confrontation in the economic field, with French resistance to the advance of American multinationals and to American designs for the reform of the international monetary system. Even before his departure from office in 1969, de Gaulle had been forced to concede defeat in many of his broad political and economic aims, but a legacy of bitterness remained. By the mid-1970s an uneasy *modus vivendi* appeared to have been established, with France as a non-conforming but relatively amenable ally in both the strategic and economic sphere; the election of a Socialist government in 1981 did little to change this picture, despite their differences with the prevailing economic theories in the 'Atlantic community'.

It can be seen that both the British pursuit of intimacy and the French repudiation of it have caused problems in transatlantic relations, both for the Americans and for others caught in the slipstream. For the West Germans, however, the progress of relations with the dominant power has been rather different again, with the initial acceptance of a necessary subordination giving way to a far more evenly balanced relationship. In the immediate postwar years it was largely through the American presence and influence that West Germany came to exist at all, with the initial occupation giving way to a merger of the British and American zones in 1947 and then to the creation of the German Federal Republic in 1949. Clearly, given the occupied status of their territory, it was difficult for West Germans to think of the kind of repudiation of American influence which could be contemplated in France; equally clearly, as it appeared to the Adenauer government in the early 1950s, the way back to international status and respectability lay through a whole-hearted acceptance of American objectives and the Atlantic Alliance. This did not mean a policy of complete passivity, however, since the West Germans could use their central position in the Cold

War confrontation to exert some leverage on even the most powerful of their allies. In the economic field espousal of European integration and pursuit of free-enterprise-led expansion of a kind much more akin to that of the United States than that of Britain or France was further evidence of the kind of creative conformity pursued by the Adenauer regime during the 1950s and early 1960s.

The period from the mid-1960s on was much less clear-cut for German–American relations. In part, this was due to the development of the broader international situation, with the erosion of American nuclear superiority and the tensions introduced into European–American relations by the French. Such developments meant that it was simply less easy for the West Germans to know which side they should be on, especially since being 'Europeanist' was no longer identical with being 'Atlanticist'. Another factor in the changing situation was American policy, which showed a tendency to treat the West Germans with a certain lack of consideration when it came to demands for the acceptance of new NATO obligations or the increasing of 'offset payments' to reduce the costs of American forces in Europe. Under the Nixon regime West German patience was taxed further by the pressure from Washington to revalue the Deutschmark as a way of reducing pressure on the dollar, and in the political field by the progress of détente – a process in which Bonn was vitally interested yet in which it often appeared to have little say.

Such trends and tensions were more important because of the growing strength of West Germans' awareness of their distinctive international needs. The phenomenon of 'self-recognition', which gained strength in the late 1960s under the government of Willy Brandt, entailed a reintroduction of legitimate political demands into West German policy. In the first place this was expressed through pursuit of *Ostpolitik* – the attempt to settle outstanding issues with the Soviet Union and other countries in Eastern Europe, which led to the various agreements of the 1972–4 period. At times this process clashed with the broader aims of American détente policy, but on the whole the two were reconciled; the more acute problems emerged when, during the 1970s, it became clear that West German leaders and their public saw détente as a continuing process while American leaderships felt it could be manipulated for political effect, with either the Soviet Union or their own public (or both) as the target.

Thanks to this uneasy coexistence of American and West German conceptions of détente, and to the continuing divergence of economic priorities between the two countries, the period beginning in 1975 and stretching into the 1980s saw considerable friction. Where the Bonn government wanted dialogue with Eastern Europe, Washington did not hesitate to proclaim a 'new Cold War'; where the Americans called for restrictions on East–West trade, the West Germans resisted, not unnaturally in view of their far greater dependence on it. Above all, the question of nuclear force modernisation aroused new controversy; the West Germans were caught between the desire to reaffirm the American commitment to 'forward defense' by the deployment of Cruise and Pershing II, and the opposition of substantial amounts of domestic opinion. From a position in the early 1970s when a German–American 'special relationship' could be seen as the logical successor to that between Britain and the United States, it appeared that, while intimate, the Bonn–Washington connection possessed a good deal of inherent conflict.

It seems clear from discussion of the British, French and West German cases that each West European country concerned has faced distinctive problems in coping with the United States – in asserting its status against the weight of a dominant power, and in reconciling the demands of European and Atlantic priorities. In the case of the fourth major West European country, Italy, the problems have been less dramatic (and less fully studied). There is considerable evidence of widespread American intervention in the Italian political process in the early postwar years, with the aim of forestalling Communist participation in the government, and this became connected with domestic political debate about adherence to the North Atlantic Treaty. Christian-Democrat-led governments during the 1950s and 1960s were concerned to demonstrate their loyalty to 'Atlanticist' conceptions of European security and integration, and until the mid-1970s there was relatively little to disturb the course of Italian–American relations. During the late 1970s and early 1980s, however, two issues did claim a good deal of attention. The first was that of Eurocommunism, and the threat that the Italian Communist Party (PCI) might come to participate in government; to this possibility the reactions of American policy-makers such as Henry Kissinger were sharply critical, although the threat never materialised.

The second contentious issue in Italian–American relations was one already noted in a number of contexts: the friction created by the new assertiveness of American claims on their allies in the early 1980s, especially through the NATO programmes for nuclear force modernisation. Although the Italian government accepted without significant opposition its quota of the projected Cruise missile force, and laid plans to station them in Sicily, there was a rapid growth of substantial domestic protest. Such protest was in line with trends in other West European countries which were to play host to the missiles (and whose governments had on the whole initially accepted their stationing). In Britain and West Germany, but also in the Netherlands, opposition was more numerous and vociferous than in Italy, and chimed with uncertainties about the newly assertive mood of broader American policies.

It was suggested at the beginning of this section that every West European country has to have a 'special relationship' with the United

States, since the dominant power is an intrusive factor in all its allies' policies. It is clear from the discussion since then that such 'special relationships' are not constant. They fluctuate in tune with the domestic pressures felt by West European governments, with the broader forces at work in the international system, and with the changes in American policy and national moods outlined at the beginning of this chapter. Lastly, it is clear that in each case the development of 'Europe' through the medium of the European Community in particular, but also within NATO, is an important modifying factor. This will now be explored in greater detail.

The Growth of 'Europe'

It could be argued that it was only with the consolidation and elaboration of links between the United States and its European allies that the idea of 'Western Europe' came to have any meaning. The Marshall Plan laid the foundations in the economic sphere, by effectively excluding Soviet-type economies and political systems from the process of American-financed reconstruction, and by encouraging initiatives on a collaborative basis through the OEEC and other bodies. In the strategic sphere NATO encapsulated the idea of 'European–American' relations as opposed to simple bilateral or more limited multilateral links, and posed for all its West European members the problem of coping with the United States strategic predominance. Although bilateral links were by no means eliminated in either the economic, the political, or the strategic realms, and indeed were important to both American and European leaderships (see above), the scene was set by the early 1950s for the development of a broader European voice in transatlantic dealings. Whether this voice proved to be positive or negative, supportive or critical of American policy, a partner or rival for influence in the world arena, it was likely to be a major factor in the conduct of European–American relations.

The strength, unity and effectiveness of a European 'caucus' in various areas of activity has not, however, been a constant or a cumulative feature of European–American affairs. Perhaps its first manifestation came in the strategic field during the very beginnings of the Cold War: the establishment, first of the Brussels Treaty and then of its permanent administrative base, which is perpetuated in the Western European Union, provided a channel for the expression of the fears felt by West European leaderships, and later for the (successful) attempt to achieve a substantial American commitment to the defence of the North Atlantic area. Even during the late 1940s, however, some of the limitations on a West European strategic voice were apparent; the defence priorities of countries such as France and the United Kingdom were often at odds, with the problem of Germany proving a fertile source of contention, and it was unclear how the weakened defence establishments of Western Europe could resist the inevitable preponderance of the United States. As already noted, the structural dominance established by the Americans in NATO extended to strategic ideas as well as organisational structures and military hardware, and this reflected in part the fragmentation of West European allies.

The impression of European weakness and fragmentation was strengthened by the failure of the European Defence Community between 1951 and 1954. If the EDC had become established as an integrated base for a European army, then a number of other developments might have been foreseen in the area of strategic doctrine and even the integration of defence industries. The demise of the plan, and the evidence that the British and French in particular cherished the idea of continued national control over defence policy and forces, meant that the idea of a concerted West European position in dealings with the United States was further off than ever. During the later 1950s both the British and the French were preoccupied with events outside Europe, or with pursuing their own 'special relationships' with the United States, while the West Germans had not yet achieved the kind of status within the Alliance which would enable them to exert more than a negative influence on events.

Such disarray at the West European end of what some Americans liked to see as a 'two-pillar' alliance meant that any kind of strategic partnership between the United States and the Europeans was bound to be fundamentally asymmetrical. While in the early 1960s the Kennedy 'grand design' set out a vision of shared responsibility for the defence of the West, this was never more than a rhetorical device. Indeed, the policies pursued by both the Kennedy administration and its successors did a great deal to forestall the emergence of any unified West European position, by emphasising the subordinate role of the European allies in general and by effectively preventing them from taking the initiative on any major strategic questions. As already noted, the attempt to implement 'flexible response' and to induce the major West European partners to play their allotted roles produced a range of responses from recalcitrance (France) through confusion (West Germany) to compliance (Britain). The one thing it seemed unlikely to produce was a consolidated West European defence posture, despite the efforts by the French to convince the West Germans of their worth as alternative allies.

On the other hand, there were during the late 1960s some movements towards the creation of a modest West European collaboration on security matters, both inside and outside NATO. Within NATO itself the tensions and recriminations which had been produced by American attempts to centralise control, and which had been aggravated by the rather clumsy attempts to promote the Multilateral Force, were defused by a broadening of consultation. The most material sign of this was the establishment of the Nuclear Planning Group, which enabled the major allies to express their views on targeting policy and general nuclear issues. Other measures were taken to promote the exchange of views between the United States and European members, but perhaps the most significant initiative was the establishment of the so-called Eurogroup; from the early 1970s this operated to promote the co-ordination of defence postures among the European members and even to introduce its own defence improvement programmes.

A number of pressures outside the formal NATO framework also conspired to produce a new European awareness during the early 1970s. One of the most important was American foreign policy, which under Nixon and Kissinger had the effect of throwing West European governments much more back on their own resources. Thus, the pursuit of détente with the Soviet Union often seemed to be carried on with less than half an eye to the possible consequences for Western Europe, and the débâcle in Vietnam provided another good reason to question the wisdom of a slavish adherence to American leadership. This trend – towards West European collaboration in the face of uncertainties about American policy – was amplified by the rather erratic nature of American leadership in the mid-1970s, and confirmed by the difficulties which arose in the 1980s over Iran, Poland and Afghanistan.

Yet the trend was somewhat paradoxical; West European governments could find common ground in their doubts about American policies, only to discover that there was little they could achieve in the way of genuine initiatives in the strategic or diplomatic field. Meanwhile, American presidents continued to act from time to time as if there was a 'Europe', especially when they were anxious for that somewhat vague entity to toe the line on Alliance questions. No issue demonstrated this more clearly than the attempt to upgrade NATO's conventional and theatre nuclear forces in the late 1970s and early 1980s; after the initial common decisions in 1979 to devote more resources to defence and to install Cruise and Pershing II missiles, the Americans came to suspect West Europeans in general of backsliding and even of incipient neutralism. In fact, the position was more complex than this implied, since the European allies were able to agree on what they did not like, and on what they might like to do about it, while proving unable in most cases to take really positive action. Additionally, there was some suspicion that the Reagan administration was prone to overlook the need for continued détente in its concentration on the acquisition of new military muscle.

What this means is that the 'West European position' on strategic questions is subtle and varied, and that it becomes more difficult to pin down the more it becomes involved with real allocations of resources rather than with rhetoric. This is not to say that there have not been important steps in European defence collaboration within NATO (such as the Italian–German–British consortium to build the Tornado aircraft, or other attempts to produce standardised weapons), but in matters of concrete military policy the Americans are always likely to retain a considerable advantage because of the relative coherence and massive weight of their strategic dispositions. Not only this, but the temptation might be – and has been – for American leaders to reject the idea of a true 'partnership' in the strategic field, and to opt instead for 'special relationships' or a 'plural' alliance system. This would, of course, have the effect of reducing or eliminating any chance of collaborative West European policies.

It was argued in Chapter 4 that the strategic alliance of the United States and Western Europe in NATO was paralleled by a kind of 'economic alliance', initiated by the Marshall Plan and carried further by the development of European economic integration. Although it is possible to see the emergence of the European Coal and Steel Community, the EEC and their associated bodies as a reflection of shared purposes within European elites, it is also clear that they reflected a strong 'Atlanticist' tinge in their early stages, not least through the beliefs of Monnet and his associates. Not only this, but also the rapid growth of policy co-ordination within the new European Communities, reflected a vigorous 'pump-priming' exercise by the United States, initially through the Marshall Plan and then through other forms of loans and financial assistance. In these circumstances co-ordination was demanded not only to chart the course of the 'new Europe' but also to administer the flow of capital, advice and assistance from across the Atlantic.

During the 1950s the dynamic benefits of sectoral integration in a recovering and expanding market, combined with the discreet encouragement of American leaderships, meant that policy co-ordination within Western Europe could benefit all concerned. While this did not make it easy to achieve, it certainly made it easier than it might have been at any other time. The only clouds on the horizon were provided by the indications (from the EDC episode) that certain sectors of political or strategic activity might prove highly resistant to any form of integration, and by the persistent ambivalence of British attitudes towards the EEC. By the end of the 1950s, though, there seemed reason to believe that even the most closely guarded areas of national sovereignty might eventually yield to the benign influence of the market and of economic growth. Economic union might thus open the door to political and strategic union in a way which might make Western Europe a fully fledged actor on the world stage.

Such an aspiration formed part of the rationale for the Kennedy administration's belief that an 'Atlantic partnership' between the United States and a uniting Europe was both desirable and possible. The belief that between them the two great Western power blocs could run not only the bulk of the world's economic system, but also the political and strategic elements of a new international order, was a seductive one, and it received a welcome in the European Commission as well as among other members of the EEC. There were, however, a variety of factors which stood in the way of unimpeded progress to 'Atlantic partnership'. As was the case with the strategic problems examined above, some of the problems arose from American policy. Although the Kennedy and Johnson administrations talked in terms of collaboration in the running of the world economy, it often appeared that they were less interested in this than in the erosion of some of the EEC's more threatening features. The Common External Tariff and the Common Agricultural Policy were seen by American business and farming interests as potentially damaging to a lucrative part of their trade, and during the early 1960s pressure mounted to break them down or dilute them. At the same time American political leaders saw 'Atlantic partnership' as a means for forcing the EEC members to bear an increased share of the burden in such areas as aid to the Third World. In the background lurked the feeling that American economic support for Western Europe had gone far enough, and that now the Europeans should collaborate as a means to pay back some of what they owed.

The response from Western Europe was mixed, to say the least. In the context of this chapter, the most important reasons for the troubles of the 1960s lay in the internal processes of the EEC and the limitations on its ability to act in any cohesive or fully representative fashion. While American interests were beginning to recognise the threat posed by a cohesive and protectionist West European bloc, the internal contradictions of European integration were operating to reduce the EEC's power of initiative – and thus its capacity to respond creatively to American pressures. By the mid-1960s the initial impetus of growth in the original 'Six' had slackened, and it was becoming clear that new levels of integration would have to be found if the dynamic benefits were to be extended into periods of slower growth. Simultaneously, it was made painfully clear that certain members of the EEC were opposed to further integration, and that they regarded the whole process as open to renegotiation or even reversal. The French under de Gaulle precipitated a major crisis in mid-1965 by refusing to accede to measures which would have increased the resources and the independence of the European Commission, and the final settlement, which was embodied in the so-called Luxembourg Compromise of 1966, stressed the intergovernmental rather than the supranational aspects of the Community's activities.

Ironically, the crisis of 1965–6 in the EEC coincided with the Community's first major confrontation with the United States, in the so-called Kennedy Round of negotiations for tariff reductions under GATT. This complex set of talks embodied part of the American determination to reduce protection in the Western world in general, but created special problems for the EEC. Although there was a commitment to a common EEC negotiating position, such a position was immensely difficult to sustain in the light of the conflicts within the 'Six'; one result was that American pressures were often met with extreme reluctance to make any changes on the part of the EEC, and an inability to make any decisions without lengthy negotiations within the Community itself. The final agreement, reached in 1967, accomplished a good deal in the way of tariff cuts, but significantly avoided any real attempt to deal with agricultural trade.

The Kennedy Round revealed a number of features of collaborative policy-making within the EEC which were to become more evident during the dramas of the late 1960s and early 1970s. First, it was clear – and became clearer – that changes in American policies provided the essential context for joint EEC action. As the collapse of the international monetary system and the 'new nationalism' of the Nixon administration became evident, the possibility existed for at least some expansion of Community policies, even if only on a defensive basis. But by a supreme irony, these opportunities occurred in precisely the circumstances which would least favour the achievement of a coherent Community position; growth was slowed, economic divergence between the members was accentuated and the politicisation of what had seemed to be largely 'technical' matters was underlined. Taken together with the effects of enlargement from six to nine members in 1973, and the intense period of negotiation which preceded the entry of Britain, Denmark and Ireland, the result was a loss of momentum on almost all the fronts of the integration process. Introspection, defensiveness and policies of an essentially reactive nature came to characterise the 'new Europe' in the years 1971–3.

By 1973, therefore, a number of important items on the West European economic agenda had been deferred if not deleted. Economic and monetary union was impossible in the context of international financial chaos and internal economic divergence, while political union had never recovered from the shocks administered by de Gaulle and was definitely not a priority for the newly 'Europeanised' British. In this context a kind of conservative paralysis set the tone of Community policy-making even before the oil price crisis of October 1973; and Henry Kissinger's call for a new effort to achieve Atlantic collaboration through the 'Year of Europe' betrayed a rather sanguine view of the Europeans' powers of initiative. The results of the pressure exerted by Kissinger were division and confusion, which dissolved into chaos under the impact of the energy shock and the unseemly scramble for assured supplies of oil.

For European–American relations the importance of politics and policy-making within the European Community lies in a paradox which has already been hinted at. The Community itself, after the shocks of the 1960s and early 1970s, is a rather untidy coalition which operates in most areas on the basis of intergovernmental politics rather than supranational administration. This means that the process of arriving at a common policy is in itself an immensely costly exercise, and that once a common stand is agreed it represents a massive investment of members' interests and influence. As a result, very often no common policy is possible; alternatively, agreed policies tend to be defensive, based on the 'lowest common denominator' of members' interests and incapable of alteration to meet changed needs. Yet this has not prevented American policy-makers from basing their approaches to the Community on expectations of a prompt 'West European' response. The result during the 1960s was often frustration and impatience on both sides; in the 1970s and 1980s it often spilled over into open hostility and recriminations.

This is not to say that there have not been areas of progress in the achievement of common 'European' policies during recent years. Where there has been progress, however, it has not always been reassuring for American policy-makers. In 1975 the Community entered into a major long-term agreement with Third World countries in the African, Caribbean and Pacific regions to stabilise trading relationships and to provide aid (the Lomé Convention). While to many this appeared to be a model for new types of aid relationship, there were fears in the United States that it might discriminate against American interests in Third World markets. Under the impact of recession, attempts have been made within the EEC to protect industries such as steelmaking which suffer from surplus capacity; again, these have aroused fears in the United States, coupled with accusations of dumping against European producers in American markets. In a third area, that of monetary policy, there has been progress of a kind through the setting up of the European Monetary System; here, too, the orientation has been primarily defensive, in this case against the instability caused by erratic movements in the price of the dollar, and it has not always met with American agreement. Finally, continued efforts to liberalise trade – or at least to prevent the spread of protectionism – under the auspices of GATT have seen confirmation of the Community members' ability to agree, but also revealed the continuing limitations of their capacity to adapt or take the initiative. Both the Tokyo Round negotiations – successors to the Kennedy Round, which concluded in 1978 – and subsequent GATT ministerial meetings saw frequent acrimony, especially on the subject of agricultural trade.

As important in many respects as the continued efforts to achieve common policies within the Community framework have been the growing intergovernmental contacts between Community members, which often produce significant results for European–American relations. The most highly developed of these contacts take place under the procedure for European Political Co-operation – a phenomenon which grew apace during the 1970s and which has no place in the Rome Treaty. Political Co-operation represents, albeit in an embryonic and explicitly intergovernmental form, an extension of Community members' interests in policy co-ordination to areas with an explicitly 'political' complexion; as such, it has brought about a number of collisions between American policy-makers and the foreign ministers of the Community, who act through the President of the Council of Ministers. The most notable of these clashes have occurred over policy towards the Arab–Israeli dispute in the Middle East, where European initiatives have consistently taken a more adventurous line on recognition of Palestinian interests than has the United States. Other areas of tension have centred on policy towards the Soviet Union and its activities in Afghanistan and Poland. It must be remembered, however, that Political Co-operation is an inherently limited exercise, and that members of the Community themselves have at various times departed from what appears to be the agreed line. All of this does not make it any easier for United States governments to cope with the 'Europeans', since it is unclear which 'rules' and procedures apply at any given time, despite the establishment of consultation devices.

It is apparent from the discussion in this section that the utterances of a 'European voice' in European–American relations have been querulous and disjointed. In the sphere of strategy the idea of a 'two-pillar' alliance seems less relevant than that of a pluralistic coalition in which a European 'caucus' coexists with 'special relationships' and with the persistence of American military dominance. In economic affairs the call for collaborative management is met by the difficulties of establishing a European position which is capable of responding to American demands, and by the unilateralism of policies on both sides of the Atlantic. The broader political sphere is penetrated by the uncertainties and lack of substance which make the voice of 'Europe' a distinctly frail instrument, and tempt Americans to discount its ability to translate declarations into substantial policies. These difficulties are not exclusive to a narrow depiction of European–American relations, however; they spill over into the more general predicament of advanced industrial societies in the contemporary international system, and must now be related to this broader set of issues.

Atlantic Institution-Building and the 'Management of Interdependence'

So far in this chapter the discussion has centred on national and collective policies in the United States and Western Europe, which have reflected the shifting structure of the Euro-American system, and which have contributed to distinct modes of action and interaction. Thus, the extension and erosion of American dominance, the waxing and waning of 'special relationships' and the emergence of a European 'caucus' within the system have been reflected in the kinds of conduct and behaviour which have been adopted with relation to particular issues and circumstances. Such a focus is useful in identifying the predicaments facing governments and policy-makers, but it also has the disadvantage of focusing attention largely on the governmental level of action. As noted in Chapter 3 especially, this is not the only level at which the environment of European–American relations can be analysed, and a great deal of attention has been paid by both academics and practitioners to the growth of contacts at non-governmental levels between the countries of the Atlantic area.

There are three major aspects to the concern with the 'management of interdependence' as a means for conducting European–American dealings. In the first place, the North Atlantic area, along with other areas of advanced industrial society such as Japan, has witnessed a massive growth in transactions carried on between societies. The expansion of travel and communications has made it possible for contacts between societies to take place more consistently and rapidly, and has also made possible the growth of new forms of industrial, commercial, or political organisations. Within the Euro-American system the activities of multinational corporations form a striking example; but it is an example which can be multiplied in many spheres of economic and cultural life. What is more, although there have been increases in economic and social linkages between societies in others parts of the world, the growth of what is commonly referred to as 'interdependence' has been concentrated in the North Atlantic area and Japan. It appears that highly industrialised, relatively 'open' societies of the type found within this part of the international system are particularly conducive to the emergence of a 'web' of cross-national dealings.

The second feature of this focus on growing interdependence is a concern for management. Increasing cross-national contacts, not all of them directly controlled by national governments, can render national mechanisms of regulation ineffective and produce damaging effects if left unchecked. Sudden or major shifts in patterns of trade, investment and production can affect many of the objectives on which governments are centred, hampering their ability to satisfy the needs of their citizens. Not only this, but the pursuit of national objectives in one issue-area can affect the fortunes of citizens in other national societies or damage the prospects of success in other issue-areas. The dangers of a loss of control are paralleled by the dangers which may result from attempts to reassert national control at the expense of others. There is thus a premium on 'managing interdependence' to maintain the benefits or reduce the damage from growing intersocietal contacts.

The incentives to 'manage', however, come up against a third factor: what might be called the 'institutional paradox'. It is assumed that the way to achieve management is through the building of institutions which reflect shared needs among the societies involved, yet the only effective way to build these institutions is on the basis of compromise between the competing objectives of national societies. Such a paradox means either that common institutions may be ill-founded and 'underpowered' or that they will be captured and used by particular national groups, among them governments. These tendencies may well be at their strongest when the obvious benefits of 'interdependence' are diluted by times of hardship or scarcity. An impressive institutional apparatus may then produce little in the way of common action or regulation, and multilateralism may give way to a 'new nationalism'.

During the twenty years after the end of the Second World War the growth of transactions between the countries involved in the Euro-American system was accompanied by the growth of a multilateral organisational framework. The Bretton Woods financial institutions had a theoretically global range, but it was between the Atlantic nations that the combination of fixed currency rates and relatively free movement of goods and capital had its most spectacular effect. In this process the IMF and the World Bank were supplemented by the Bank for International Settlements, which gave European and American central banks an important role in maintaining the integrity of the system. Meanwhile, the mechanism of GATT could be used to ensure the multilateral and relatively 'free' nature of trading practices between the industrial nations. It appeared that the conduct of Atlantic economic relations was thus based on principles of non-discrimination and multilateralism, and that the growth of wealth in the North Atlantic area generally would provide the institutional framework with a continuing legitimacy. The transformation of the OEEC into the OECD in the early 1960s seemed to symbolise this trend, since it associated the United States and the other Western industrial states on a basis of multilateralism and equality. At the same time the high level of official contacts between governmental departments in the United States and Western Europe, and the activities of multinational business, seemed to provide an even broader foundation for the management of common problems; a 'transgovernmental' and a 'transnational' cement seemed to bind the Euro-American system ever more firmly together.

As with so many other aspects of European–American affairs, it was during the 1960s that this vision began to tarnish. The 'multilateralism' of the 1950s was difficult to separate from American economic predominance, as has already been noted at several points, and the willingness of West European societies to open themselves up to the vagaries of 'interdependence' can be seen as a symptom of their subordination rather than their commitment to an 'open' world order. As the 1960s proceeded it began to appear that far from being an answer to the problems of economic growth, 'interdependence' *was* the problem. For West Europeans two symptoms were especially acute: first, the fact that the United States position as a kind of 'banker' for the financial and monetary system seemed to give American policy-makers a means to blackmail their allies in a variety of spheres; and secondly, the effects which seemed to flow from the peaceful 'invasion' by American multinational business. Mobility of capital and technological expertise seemed to attack the roots of European statehood by eroding the control exercised by governments over their macroeconomic policies, and this at a time when some of the major West European governments were attempting to reassert their national status.

This meant that the mechanisms of multilateral management began to come under increasing pressure. To some (including General de Gaulle) it appeared that such legitimacy as these institutions had achieved was essentially conditional; with the decline of American dominance, and the resurgence of national confidence in Western Europe, they should be recast to reflect the new 'balance of power', just as in the strategic sphere NATO should be remodelled. GATT (in the Kennedy Round) and the IMF (in the currency crises of the late 1960s) became arenas for political competition rather than economic management, and the OECD remained unable to take positive measures affecting the economic strategies of its members. Nor was the EEC able to play a major role in redressing the balance, given that its own institutions were now regarded as contestable and manipulable by its major members.

One essential element of the 'management of interdependence', according to Miriam Camps, is the development among the countries concerned of a common vision of the future of the international system. Without such a shared image, institutions and procedures are likely to become contested and to be used more as tools of their members' policies than as the seed-bed for genuine transformation. By the end of the 1960s in European–American relations, under the impact of American uncertainties and West European fragmentation, it appeared that there were as many different futures as there were national societies contemplating them. In these circumstances the entry of Britain into the EEC, which had been seen by earlier enthusiasts as a precondition for genuine 'partnership' in the international order, made little impact; in fact, by causing EEC members to become preoccupied with putting their own house in some kind of order, it seemed further to dilute the chances of multilateralism. American policies – most starkly expressed in the 'Nixon Shock' of August 1971, but more broadly pointing to a 'new nationalism' in the dominant economy of the Euro-American system – again constituted a repudiation of some of the most hallowed precepts of the 'interdependence' theology.

The assumed virtues of multilateral management and institution-building were given what to many seemed a terminal shock by the oil price crisis of 1973–5. Not only was this a threat to supplies of a commodity vital to industrial societies; it also greatly accentuated preexisting levels of economic divergence between the advanced industrial countries, and it completed the destruction of the Bretton Woods system. To the casual observer this might have implied the death of international management, but such has not been the case; rather, the mechanisms of regulation and adjustment have taken different forms, some more and some less effective, to deal with new conditions. The message of the past ten years seems to be that the 'management of interdependence' is more necessary than ever, but that it is unlikely to be achieved through elaborate institutions or the formal rules they might enshrine.

One symptom of this new form of management consists of what might be called 'crisis measures'. The oil price crisis − and subsequent energy shocks in the late 1970s − spawned the International Energy Agency, under the aegis of the OECD, which has a narrowly defined responsibility for co-ordinating its members' responses to disruptions in oil supplies. Quite apart from this formal mechanism, there have grown up a set of practices which express the accumulated wisdom of Atlantic countries in dealing with economic shocks − in the monetary sphere with the 'recycling' of Arab oil wealth or the handling of 'bad debts', in the trade sphere with the practice of consultation over particular forms of threats to established markets or producers, and in the sphere of macroeconomic policy with the so-called 'Western Economic Summits' and their preparatory activities. These mechanisms are on the whole less formal and permanent than the more traditional institutions of management, and they also frequently involve activities by non-governmental agencies such as banks or corporations.

Even where such measures as these are promoted, however, it is clear that in the 1980s the idea of multilateral management faces severe difficulties. One of the most obvious of these is the obstacle posed by domestic forces in the economic field; demands for protection or support may severely circumscribe the freedom of manoeuvre available to governments in the international sphere, and this tendency can be accentuated by the growth of legislative interest in what have been termed 'intermestic' affairs. As a consequence, and as illustrated by several of the 'Western Economic Summits', declarations of a symbolic nature, which can readily be espoused by leaders meeting well away from the domestic 'audience', may never have any practical impact. During the late 1970s attempts to impress on the West Germans and Japanese their responsibility for leading the world out of recession met a dusty response, as did efforts to influence the course of domestic American energy policies.

Equally important during the early 1980s, and perhaps more ominous in the long run for the future of European–American relations, is evidence that governments may set out deliberately to use 'interdependence' either to punish or to impose costs on others. At its most extreme, this can involve the use of economic sanctions to exploit the vulnerability of those in a dependent position. More subtle forms of the practice can entail manipulation of the 'rules' or indirect discrimination so that others are forced to bear the costs of adjustment to new circumstances. Such practices are by no means new in European–American dealings, but in 1981 and 1982 they seemed at times to form a dominant form of conduct. On the one hand, President Reagan threatened the European subsidiaries of American multinationals with penalties if they supplied materials for the Soviet–Western Europe gas pipeline, while continuing to offer grain supplies to Moscow. On the other hand, West European responses to the threat of Japanese 'invasion' of certain markets and the pursuit of 'managed trading agreements' appeared to divert the threat to the United States (which itself was attempting the same strategy). Legal action was threatened on all sides to constrain the dumping of surplus products, and there seemed more of a commitment to litigation and self-defence than to a 'common vision of the future'.

'Interdependence', or different levels of dependence, are clearly more difficult to 'manage' in the Euro-American system in the 1980s than they were in the 1950s. A variety of factors seems to account for this change, among them the impact of recession and the decline of tangible benefits to be gained from accepting the risks entailed. Once again, it is clearly important that the changed position of the United States in the system has led to an erosion of its leaders' ability or inclination to sustain the established order, without the emergence of other potential 'managers'. As has been stressed above, however, a great deal of management still goes on within the European–American arena; just because it does not fit the seductive vision of a unified Atlantic Community, that does not compromise its effectiveness. What might compromise its effectiveness is the development of introspective, defensive and neo-nationalist policies on both sides of the Atlantic. As has been argued here, there is a host of problems to which that is no answer at all.

From the discussion in this chapter it should be clear that the conduct of European–American relations takes place at many levels and with many modes of activity. Given the proliferation of institutions and interested groups at both the governmental and non-governmental levels within the Atlantic area, it would be surprising if the ways in which transatlantic business is conducted did not reflect at least some of this resulting complexity. What is perhaps more important for the argument here is that traces at least of all the ways in which European–American relations have been conducted since 1945 are still visible; in theory, all of the 'traditional' channels of communication and influence are still available alongside the 'new'. As a result, the several different sets of 'rules' and codes of conduct' for transatlantic dealings exist in an uneasy and shifting balance.

In simple terms, this situation poses for policy-makers the fundamental question 'how should we behave ourselves?' Put in a slightly more sophisticated way, it appears that in framing their actions, and in attempting to resolve disputes or to sustain collaborative ventures, leaders in both the United States and Western Europe have had available to them a range of tried and trusted and relatively novel mechanisms; the problem has increasingly been that there are no obvious guidelines as to which (singly or in combination) are likely to work. Thus, the United States hegemony may not be what it once was, but it is still tempting for American leaders to pursue the 'politics of dominance'; the 'special relationships' of old may now be strained, but the assumptions and suspicions they conjured up are still with us. Further problems have been created by the disparity between the EEC's anticipated (or feared) implications and its no less challenging reality. The 'management of interdependence' may have been confined to increasingly limited aspirations in the 1970s and 1980s but none the less expresses a continuing imperative for the societies involved. It is logical to conclude that such difficulties reflect the substance of relations as exposed in earlier chapters – the intimately shared environments and the contested issue-areas of the Euro-American system. As a result, both for policy-makers and for academic analysts, there exists a double danger: first, that expectations will be confounded by essentially unpredictable outcomes; and secondly, that the significance of change within the system will be extraordinarily difficult to gauge.

Further Reading

The debate about appropriate methods for the conduct of European–American relations has fluctuated over the period since 1945, and has a strong policy orientation as well as an analytical focus. The following general treatments of Atlantic relations cover many of the issues dealt with in this chapter, and are also revealing about the assumptions and debating-points which were current at the time of their publication: Chace and Ravenal (1976); Czempiel and Rustow (1976); Hahn and Pfaltzgraff (1979); Hanrieder (1974); and Wilcox and Haviland (1963).

On the more specific areas covered here, the following should be seen.

American hegemony and its erosion: For the general issue, see especially: Calleo (1970, 1982); Calleo and Rowland (1973); and Kaldor (1979). On the problem of changes in American leadership and policy stability, see: Hoffmann (1968, 1978); Kissinger (1960, 1965); Osgood *et al.* (1973); Oye (1979); Rosecrance (1976); Tucker (1981); Vernon (1973); and Whitman (1975). More limited treatments (because they are either linked to a specific period of time or to a specific issue-area) can be found in: Cromwell (1978); Fox and Fox (1967); Garnett (1968); Kohl (1975); Kolko and Kolko (1972); and Kraft (1962).

'Special relationships': The three major areas of concentration here are France,

West Germany and the United Kingdom. In general terms, Fox and Schilling (1973, esp. on the security problem) and Grosser (1980, esp. on France and Germany) are most useful. On France in particular, see: Cleveland (1966); Furniss (1953, 1956, 1961); Harrison (1981); Kohl (1971); and Zahnser (1975). West Germany attracted much attention especially during the 1970s. On the relationship in general, Adenauer (1966), Kelleher (1975), Morgan (1974), Richardson (1966) and Willis (1968) are helpful. For the 1970s and 1980s, see: Dönhoff (1979); Gatzke (1980); Glass (1979); Griffith (1982); Johnson (1979); Kaiser (1978); and Storey (1981). The British–American relationship was more studied during the 1960s, reflecting its salience in general. See especially: Bell (1964); Camps (1960); Manderson-Jones (1972); Neustadt (1970); and for the 1970s and 1980s, Smith (1981).

The 'European caucus': In general, see: Calleo (1965); Feld (1978); Harrison (1974); Kleiman (1964); Kolodziej (1980–1); and Servan-Schrieber (1968). More limited to the EEC are: Camps (1967, 1971); Diebold (1960); Mally (1974); and Schaetzel (1975). On particular issues, the following are a sample: Burrows and Edwards (1982); Casadio (1973); Holmes (1968); and Preeg (1970).

The 'management of interdependence': The question in general is addressed by: Ball (1974, an early version of the problem); Camps (1974); Cooper (1968); and Kaiser (1973). The specific area of institution-building is covered (with special reference to the OECD) in: Aubrey (1967); Camps (1975); Gordon (1956a); and Henderson (1981). (See also materials on the EEC cited above.) Problems emerging from the growth of interconnectedness are explored by: Cooper (1972–3); Diebold (1980); Malmgren (1970–1); Oye et al.(1979, esp. essay by Keohane); Wallace (1976); and Walton (1976).

Conclusions

European–American relations are simultaneously important and intractable, and anyone who claims to have unlocked all their secrets is either a fool or a knave. Both the operations of decision-makers and academic investigations fall foul of the consistently puzzling and contradictory nature of the Euro-American system, as indicated in Chapter 2 of this study. In very crude terms, the book has attempted to cope with two questions raised in Part One: first, what has changed and what has persisted in European–American relations?; and secondly, what precisely are the problems faced by practitioners and analysts in attempting to think clearly about the field? By attempting in a modest way to identify some of the major dimensions of the Euro-American system, Part Two may at least have provided the basis for a more searching pursuit of such questions – perhaps even for some partial and tentative answers.

The issue of continuity and change is approached from different angles in each of Chapters 3–5. Thus, a focus on the setting of European–American relations alerts the reader to a process of continuous transformation at the global, regional and national levels; but it also uncovers areas of substantial continuity in the underlying structures and forces within which action takes place. On the one side, the 'open' nature of the Euro-American system exposes its members to a range of influences from the global environment; yet at the same time, the shifting balance of forces within the system, at the Atlantic, West European, or national levels, has generated its own incentives and constraints. In a somewhat similar way, the 'agenda' of issues in European–American relations – strategic, economic and political – has remained broadly consistent throughout the postwar period, yet no one could claim that the ways in which the issues are defined or fought out have been uniform. Fluctuating perceptions of commitment and obligation, willingness or unwillingness to bear the cost of involvement and greater or lesser degrees of consensus and pluralism have all been noticeable. When it comes to the conduct of relations within the Euro-American system, the coexistence of the traditional and the novel presents decision-makers with problems of co-ordination and choice which sometimes defy the logic of a broadly stable set of expectations and assumptions. Knowing how to behave – and how to frame expectations of others' behaviour – in an untidy and changing context thus becomes a major potential source of uncertainty.

Such a judgement leads on naturally to a reappraisal of the policy-making 'puzzle'. In Chapter 2 it was argued that European–American relations tempted policy-makers to pronounce general doctrines or designs while ensuring that such pronouncements came to a sticky end. The discussion in Chapters 3–5 shows that this paradox is almost a necessary element of the Euro-American system. Doctrines and pronouncements, it appears, respond to the changing setting of transatlantic relations: at various times they have expressed a perceived need for solidarity against external threat, the exertion of dominance by certain members of the system (or the attempt to stem decline) and the contest between opposed camps within a shifting balance of forces. The attempt to impose a 'design' can also be seen as a symptom of the increasing pluralism and internal contradictions within the system; in fact, the 'image' of European–American relations has at various times been a major 'agenda item', a focus for contention and confrontation. Finally, the whole notion of a shared (or imposed) view on the nature of the Euro-American system is inseparable from the 'code of conduct' or 'weapons of combat' which enable business to be carried on within the system. Partly, this may reflect an atavistic yearning by some policy-makers for a 'golden age' when everyone behaved themselves and played by the rules (real or imagined). Partly, also, it may be a natural response to an uncertain and changing setting and an attempt to justify policy to doubting domestic or international audiences. Whatever the case may be, it is clear that the relationship between policy-makers' words and the reality of the Euro-American system is an important indicator of the system's evolution.

Finally, what of the second 'puzzle' identified in Chapter 2? One conclusion which is easy to reach is that all of the academic perspectives dealt with there have something to offer, while none of them approaches a complete description of European–American relations (let alone an explanation). An approach based on 'power and security' is thus very effective in pointing out the persistence of many of the basic structures which support the Euro-American system – and in underlining the importance of American–Soviet relations as a major element in the context. Such an approach also highlights the 'security dilemmas' which underlie the trials and tribulations of NATO, and reinforces the impression that a major element in the changing 'rules of the game' for both Americans and West Europeans has been the erosion of American leadership. A 'power and security' approach, however, is not very sensitive to the growth of economic and social connections between the United States and Western Europe, which clearly constitute a major feature of the changing setting. Such connections are better discerned through the use of an 'interdependence' framework, which also draws attention to the linkages between domestic and international aspects of the Euro-American system, and to the increasing salience of international institutions as a means of conducting relations. This kind of analysis is taken further by the 'integration and community-building' approach, which stresses the mutual responsiveness of groups and elites within the system and adds a quasi-ideology of 'Atlanticism' to the picture. The difficulty for both 'interdependence' and 'integration' approaches, as can be illustrated from the arguments in Chapters 3–5, is that there are important questions which they either cannot answer or 'take as read'. The persistence (and fluctuation) of the Soviet threat, the varying extent of American dominance and leadership and the questionable nature of 'Western Europe' as a component of Atlantic relations are only three of these issues, yet each is central to a full comprehension of the Euro-American system. Equally important – and stressed by those who see the building and break-up of an American 'empire' – is the fact that there are real differences of interests and important structural conflicts within the system, arising from the shifting foundations of dominance and dependence. The conflicts cannot be denied at the broad structural level, yet they are confused, muted and often compromised at the level of strategy or the day-to-day business of Atlantic relations.

It thus appears that no school of thought has a monopoly on the field of European–American relations. Nor could it be otherwise, given the essentially contestable nature of much of the Euro-American system as it has been explored in this book and the closeness of academic analysis to the real world of policy. The arguments put forward here have been designed to highlight problems which have to be confronted no matter what academic approach or practical project is to be pursued. What cannot be contested is that for the foreseeable future European–American relations will matter greatly. The analyst is thus condemned to live permanently in the midst of great events and to discern their proportions only dimly. Perhaps this book will illuminate one or two corners at least.

Table. The Members of the Euro-American System

	1	2	3	4	Membership of:		
	Territory (000s km^2)	Population (m.) (end-1980)	Gross National Product per capita (US$) (1978)	Armed Forces (000s) (total, 1982)	OECD	EEC	NATO
Belgium	30·519	9·863	9,700	93·5	★	★	★
Denmark	43·076	5·123	10,580	31·2	★	★	★
France	547·026	53·838	8,880	492·9	★	★	—[a]
GFR	248·667	61·658	10,300	495·0	★	★	★
Greece	131·990	9·706	3,450	206·5	★	★	★
Ireland	17·367	3·368 (1979 Census)	3,810	16·4	★	★	—
Italy	301·263	57·140	4,600	370·0	★	★	★
Luxembourg	2·586	0·365	11,320	0·7	★	★	★
Netherlands	33·940	14·208	9,200	104·0	★	★	★
Norway	323·895	4·092	9,560	42·1	★	—[b]	★
Portugal	92·072	9·933	1,940	66·4	★	—[b]	★
Spain	504·782	37·552	3,960	347·0	★	—	★
Turkey	779·452	44·700	1,250	569·0	★	—	★
United Kingdom	244·103	55·944 (1980 Census)	5,720	327·6	★	★	★
United States	9,363·123	227·640	9,770	2,116·8	★	—	★

★ Indicates membership.

Notes: (a) Subscribes to North Atlantic Treaty but not a member of integrated command.
(b) Applicant for EEC membership (as of 1983).

Sources: Cols. 1–3 Europa Yearbook 1982, London, Europa, 1982. Population figures are official estimates unless otherwise stated. Gross National Product figures are not always strictly comparable.
Col. 4 The Military Balance 1982–3 (London: International Institute for Strategic Studies, 1983).

Bibliography

Introduction

As noted at many points in this book, European–American relations have been central both to the development of the international system in general and to the concerns of policy-makers. These two factors account in large measure for the nature of the literature in the area, which is rich, diverse and extensive. It would have been possible in principle to construct a bibliography as long as the book itself, but the purpose of the present effort is more modest. The items gathered together here are thus intended, individually and collectively, to reflect the development of academic and policy-making approaches within the context of Atlantic relations; each of them is significant in some way as a 'symptom' of or a comment upon the underlying patterns stressed in the text. The annotations are designed to indicate both the content of the items and their relationship to major themes outlined in the book.

Although the bibliography includes only selected documentary and periodical references, it is useful briefly to comment in general on the major sources for the study of this area. One point which should be made at once is that in the study of European–American relations the distinction between a 'primary' document and a 'secondary' article or book is often blurred, since the 'semi-official' periodicals and series often have a historical value of their own, relating to debates among policy-making elites in both Europe and the United States. Another point to note is that 'proper' historical documentation about the later parts of the period dealt with is very hard to come by, given national practices in relation to the release of official documents. What is gained from the continuing semi-public airing of elite views in various contexts is therefore constrained through the 'thirty year' and other rules, but the result is still a massive resource for the historian and the social scientist. For the 1940s and early 1950s, a start has been made by several authors who have assembled collections of documents; for later periods, there are one or two collections of publicly available documentation. Examples of both types appear in the main bibliography below.

In terms of 'official' documentary sources and surveys, there are three major series which serve analysts of European–American relations. First, the United States Department of State produces annual reviews of *Foreign Relations of the United States*, collecting documents and statements of policy, and including a review of Atlantic relations. Secondly, the Council on Foreign Relations, a private but well-connected body in New York, produces a series of *Documents on American Foreign Relations*, which overlaps with but does not duplicate the State Department's efforts. Finally, the Royal Institute of International Affairs in London produced a major series of *Documents in International Affairs* to accompany its annual *Survey of International Affairs* (for years up to 1963 only, unfortunately). Each of these sources has its merits and defects; perhaps their most obvious limitation is the one which finally did for the RIIA *Survey* – they often run in arrears by several years.

This means that less ambitious and more topical 'official publications' are often more readily available and useful. Here again, the State Department is a major contributor with its monthly *Bulletin*, which contains a mixture of comment and analysis as well as texts of speeches, agreements, and so on. The European Community's *Official Journal*, published monthly, is an essential source for the doings of Community bodies, but suffers as a result of its comprehensive nature as a 'journal of record'. Two other organisations produce periodicals: first, the OECD, which publishes its *Observer* six times a year with accompanying editions of the *Economic Outlook* (every six months); these are invaluable as sources of data and analysis on the 'Atlantic economy'. More obviously a 'public relations' publication is the *Review* published by NATO (also bi-monthly).

The academic journals in the field can usefully be assessed in terms of their proximity to the concerns of policy-makers, and also their topicality. On both sides of the Atlantic there are a number of periodicals which are very close to the 'policy-making community' and which often reflect debates going on within that group. In the United States three such journals are particularly notable: first, *Foreign Affairs*, which is published quarterly (with an additional review of *America and the World* annually since 1979) by the Council on Foreign Relations in New York. The pages of this journal have frequently witnessed debates (and pitched battles on occasion) over American policies in Europe: 'disengagement' in the late 1950s, the 'grand design' and the crises of the 1970s and 1980s are all to be found there, often engaging the views and arguments of officials and policy-makers. In rather the same way, *Orbis* (produced by the Foreign Policy Research Institute in Philadelphia, quarterly) covers mainly strategic and security issues. More obviously 'official' is the *Atlantic Community Quarterly*, produced by the Atlantic Council of the United States, which focuses on the North Atlantic area and on NATO in particular. Less 'establishment' than any of the above is the quarterly *Foreign Policy*, which sets itself the brief of being critical and exploring alternatives in American policy, and has fostered a number of seminal debates about the new challenges of the 1970s and 1980s.

On the 'European' side, two institutes produce journals which provide debate and documentation: first, the Royal Institute of International Affairs in London, whose quarterly *International Affairs* is more 'academic' than *Foreign Affairs*, but often contains illuminating material from policy-makers or well-informed academics. The Institute also produces a more topical monthly journal, *The World Today*, which gathers together a diverse collection of contributions from journalists, officials and academics on contemporary issues. The International Institute for Strategic Studies produces a bi-monthly periodical, *Survival*, which reflects current debate in the 'strategic studies community' and also reprints important official statements or documents on military affairs, many of which relate to European–American relations.

The more 'academic' and theoretical journals in international relations and economics also pay frequent attention to issues of European–American relations. *The World Economy*, published quarterly by the Trade Policy Research Centre in association with Basil Blackwell (Oxford), generates a considerable amount of discussion especially on trade and monetary policy. The *Journal of Common Market Studies*, published by Blackwell in association with the University Association for Contemporary European Studies (three issues per year), deals with theoretical and empirical studies of integration which often have implications for the Atlantic area. *International Organization*, an American quarterly published under the auspices of the World Peace Foundation since 1945, had a very strong 'Atlantic' orientation during its early years; since about 1965 this has changed in favour of a strong orientation towards global interdependence issues, but there are still quite frequent items relating to the 'advanced industrial societies'. On the strategic studies side, *International Security*, published quarterly by Harvard College, contains a valuable mixture of theoretical and current debate (rather in the same way as *Orbis*, see above, but less obviously policy-oriented). The most recently established of all journals in the field is the *Atlantic Quarterly* (first published 1983), which appears likely to be very useful to students of the area.

Although they do not count as periodicals or journals, it is worth noting that a number of the institutes already mentioned have produced series of books or monographs related to problems of European–American relations. The Council on Foreign Relations has produced two major series: in the mid-1960s it started the *Atlantic Policy Studies*, an enterprise which brought together many influential and well-informed commentators and which attempted to assess the development and future of the 'Atlantic Community'. During the late 1970s a new series of studies were produced under the aegis of the *1980s Project*; this reflected an analysis based more on interdependence and globalism than on alliance politics and the Atlantic area, but provided equally valuable material. The 'Atlantic' focus has been pursued diligently by the Atlantic Institute, based in Boulogne-sur-Seine (France), which has generated a lengthy series of *Atlantic Papers*. The Royal Institute of International Affairs has sponsored many studies of Atlantic problems, most recently as part of its series of *Chatham House Papers* (published in association with Routledge & Kegan Paul); these cover in monograph form a variety of economic, strategic and political issues. A more longstanding series of monographs is the International Institute for Strategic Studies' *Adelphi Papers* – by 1983 nearly 200 had been published, many of them reflecting European–American debates.

A final note on sources for 'updating' on current events: a number of weekly magazines are valuable, especially *The Economist* and *Newsweek*; newspapers of particular relevance include *Le Monde diplomatique*, the *New York Times*, *The Times* and the *Guardian*, all of which devote considerable news and features space to Atlantic relations. Any research on contemporary European–American problems would be lost without such materials, in addition to those indicated earlier.

Select List of Books and Articles

Acheson, D. (1970), *Present at the Creation: My Years in the State Department* (London: Hamish Hamilton). The memoirs of a secretary of state (1949–52) who was at the centre of the Marshall Plan and NATO developments. Especially interesting on the evolution of American strategies and attitudes in Western Europe.

Adenauer, K. (1966), *Memoirs, 1945–1953* (London: Weidenfeld & Nicolson). Very important to an understanding of West German views on NATO, the occupation and recovery of sovereignty.

Alting von Geusau, F. (ed.)(1983), *Allies in a Turbulent World: Challenges to US and Western European Cooperation* (Lexington, Mass.: D. C. Heath). A very interesting collection, covering foreign policy co-operation, strategic problems and economic issues (although the last are less well covered than the others).

Artner, S. (1980), 'The Middle East: a chance for Europe?', *International Affairs*, vol. 56, no. 3, pp. 420–42. Argues that although basic interests of the United States and Western Europe are parallel, differences in historical experience and current capabilities need to be overcome.

Art, R. (1982), 'Fixing Atlantic bridges', *Foreign Policy*, no. 46, pp. 67–85. An effective review of the continuing rationale for NATO, but also one which stresses the need for acceptance of more pluralism and consultation in the Alliance.

Aubrey, H. (1967), *Atlantic Economic Co-operation: The Case of the OECD* (New York: Praeger for Council on Foreign Relations). One of the spate of books which focused on the growth of an 'Atlantic Community', and one of the few on the OECD itself as an institution.

Ball, G. (1982), *The Past Has Another Pattern: Memoirs* (New York: W. W. Norton). Ball is one of the great 'Atlanticists', a close ally of Monnet and involved in many of the seminal movements of the 1950s and 1960s. The memoirs are tinged slightly with wishful thinking, but often are revealing.

Ball, M. M. (1974), *NATO and the European Union Movement* (Westport, Conn.: Greenwood Press). Originally published in 1960; a major early attempt to see the links and tensions between the Alliance and the emerging EEC.

Bell, C. (1964), *The Debatable Alliance: An Essay in Anglo-American Relations* (London: Oxford University Press for Royal Institute of International Affairs). A study of the 'special relationship' which is especially interesting in the light of British approaches to the EEC in the late 1950s and early 1960s, but which focuses mainly on strategic issues.

Beloff, M. (1976), *The United States and the Unity of Europe* (Westport, Conn.: Greenwood Press). Another reprint of an early 'classic', this one originally published in 1963. Beloff is most interesting on the shifts in American policy which produced the postwar involvement in Europe, and reveals the ambivalence of American 'Atlanticism'.

Benoit, E. M. (1961), *Europe at Sixes and Sevens: The Common Market, the Free Trade Area and the United States* (New York: Columbia University Press). Benoit is especially interesting on the likely economic costs and benefits of developments in Western Europe, and generally stresses the opportunities for American business expansion.

Bergsten, C. F. (1981), 'The costs of Reaganomics', *Foreign Policy*, no. 44, pp. 24–36. One of a number of critics who pointed to the damaging effects of American macroeconomic policy on the 'Atlantic economy' during the early 1980s.

van der Beugel, E. (1966), *From Marshall Aid to Atlantic Partnership: European Integration as a Concern of American Policy* (Amsterdam: Elsevier). A most interesting treatment, particularly in the view it gives of the origins of NATO and the Marshall Plan (van der Beugel was closely involved in the setting up of the OEEC and the 'selling' of the European Recovery Programme).

Brzezinski, Z. (1965), *Alternative to Partition: For a Broader Conception of the American Role in Europe* (New York: McGraw-Hill for Council on Foreign Relations). Draws attention to the erosion of the Eastern bloc and the possibilities this creates for an American initiative aimed at 'peaceful engagement'.

Buchan, A. (1960), *NATO in the 1960s: The Implications of Interdependence* (London: Chatto & Windus). A most important source for those concerned to understand changes in European views and the response to American alliance policies.

Buchan, A. (1962–3), 'Europe and the Atlantic Alliance: two strategies or one?', *Journal of Common Market Studies*, vol. 1, no. 3, pp. 224–55. Reflects the strategic aspect of debates on 'Atlantic Community' at the time.

Buchan, A. (1964), 'The MLF: a study in alliance politics', *International Affairs*, vol. 40, no. 4, pp. 619–37. One of the most accessible and succinct studies of the MLF issue.

Bundy, McG., Kennan, G., McNamara, R., and Smith, G. (1982), 'Nuclear weapons and the Atlantic Alliance', *Foreign Affairs*, vol. 60, no. 4, pp. 753–68. One of the central contributions to the debate over NATO strategy, in particular the idea of 'first use' of nuclear weapons (it argues that a 'no first use' pledge would be a major contribution to Alliance cohesion and strategic stability).

Burrows, B., and Edwards, G. (1982), *The Defence of Western Europe* (London: Butterworth). Deals with military and non-military aspects of the problem; and argues for a West European 'identity', but within a firmly Atlantic framework.

Calleo, D. (1965), *Europe's Future: The Grand Alternatives* (New York: Horizon Press). Sets out a number of possible patterns for Europe – only some of which are 'Atlantic' in orientation. An interesting exercise, which stresses links of economic, political and strategic issues.

Calleo, D. (1970), *The Atlantic Fantasy: The US, NATO and Europe* (Baltimore, Md, and London: Johns Hopkins University Press). Argues strongly that American 'Atlanticism' is a facade for domination, and that a more equal partnership of Western Europe and the United States should be established.

Calleo, D. (1982), *The Imperious Economy* (Cambridge, Mass.: Harvard University Press). The most recent manifestation of Calleo's longstanding argument that American self-centredness and introspection have damaged the world and Western economies.

Calleo, D., and Rowland, B. (1973), *America and the World Political Economy: Atlantic Dreams and National Realities* (Bloomington, Ind., and London: Indiana State University Press). Carries further the argument first made in *The Atlantic Fantasy*, but with particular reference to trade, monetary issues, and ideas of 'community' and integration.

Camps, M. (1960), 'Britain, the Six and American policy', *Foreign Affairs*, vol. 39, no. 1, pp. 112–22. Exposes the central position of the United Kingdom in any 'partnership' of the United States and Western Europe.

Camps, M. (1967), *European Unification in the Sixties; From the Veto to the Crisis* (London: Oxford University Press for Royal Institute of International Affairs). This was also published as part of the Council on Foreign Relations' *Atlantic Policy Studies* series. It has a particularly interesting final section on 'The American interest in European integration' which sums up a lot of the emergent problems of the 1960s.

Camps, M. (1971), 'European unification in the Seventies', *International Affairs*, vol. 47, no. 4, pp. 671–8. Points to the emergence of the EEC as something more than the sum of its parts, yet less than a full international 'actor', and questions its relevance to some of the developing problems in the setting of the 1970s.

Camps, M. (1972), 'Sources of strain in transatlantic relations', *International Affairs*, vol. 48, no. 4, pp. 559–78. Traces the first rumblings of what was to become the major crisis of the mid-1970s.

Camps, M. (1974), *The Management of Interdependence: A Preliminary View* (New York: Council on Foreign Relations). The 'foundation-stone' of the Council's *1980s Project*, and important because it states very firmly the case for co-ordination of advanced industrial societies' policies in the face of increasingly global problems.

Camps, M. (1975), *'First World' Relationships: The Role of the OECD*, Atlantic Papers (Boulogne-sur-Seine: Atlantic Institute). Reflects the feeling that the OECD could be a more effective vehicle for policy co-ordination and co-operation, but also a view of its inevitable limitations.

Casadio, G. (1973), *Transatlantic Trade: USA–EEC Confrontation in the GATT Negotiations* (Farnborough: Saxon House). Sets out the issues which arose during the Kennedy Round, as well as those which were to be central to later GATT negotiations.

Chace, J., and Ravenal, E. (eds)(1976), *Atlantis Lost: The United States and Europe after the Cold War* (New York: New York University Press for Council on Foreign Relations). Crammed full of good articles by Calleo, Hoffmann, Pierre, Morse and many others, most of whom expressed a kind of 'disillusioned Atlanticism' compounded by failings on the part of the Americans and the Europeans.

Clay, L. (1950), *Decision in Germany* (New York: Doubleday). Clay was commander of the American occupation forces, and this memoir contains much valuable material on the evolution of American attitudes towards a 'presence' in Western Europe.

Cleveland, H. van B. (1966), *The Atlantic Idea and its European Rivals* (New York: McGraw-Hill for Council on Foreign Relations). One of the 'keynote' volumes for the *Atlantic Policy Studies*. Sets out and contrasts American and European (especially French) attitudes.

Cohen, B. (1979), 'Europe's money, America's problem', *Foreign Policy*, no. 35, pp. 31–47. Assesses the problems caused by the fluctuations of the dollar, and the prospects for the European Monetary System.

Coker, C. (1982), 'The Western Alliance and Africa, 1949–1981', *African Affairs*, vol. 81, no. 324, pp. 319–35. One of the very few analyses of this problem, revealing the caution displayed by NATO towards 'out of area operations'.

Cooper, R. N. (1968), *The Economics of Interdependence: Economic Policy in the Atlantic Community* (New York: McGraw-Hill for Council for Foreign Relations). A major study in two ways. First, it sets out what ought to happen within the Bretton Woods system of financial and monetary institutions; and secondly, it shows how the growth of transactions and interconnections has eroded the control of governments and thus their ability to 'play by the rules' even if they want to.

Cooper, R. N. (1972–3), 'Trade policy is foreign policy', *Foreign Policy*, no. 9, pp. 18–36. Traces the growing use of trade in foreign policy, and the growing impact of trading needs on the making of policy.

Cromwell, W. (1978), 'Europe and the "Structure of Peace" ', *Orbis*, vol. 22, no. 1, pp. 11–36. Evaluates the Nixon–Kissinger design for a new world balance, and the tensions this implied for the role of Western Europe.

Cromwell, W. (ed.)(1969), *Political Problems of Atlantic Partnership: National Perspectives* (Bruges: College of Europe). The first essay, by Cromwell himself, is a valuable study of American aims and their internal contradictions as illustrated by the events of the 1960s.

Czempiel, E-O., and Rustow, D. (eds)(1976), *The Euro-American System* (Frankfurt: Campus-Verlag; Boulder, Colo: Westview Press). Sets out to describe and explain the workings of the 'system', but many of the contributors are rather sceptical that it exists or can ever exist. It is valuable as a mid-1970s indicator of 'Atlanticism'.

DePorte, A. W. (1979), *Europe between the Superpowers: The Enduring Balance* (New Haven, Conn., and London: Yale University Press). Although not confined to Western Europe, this is one of the most valuable studies of the 'power and security' aspects of postwar developments. DePorte argues that during the 1940s and 1950s a new 'state system' emerged in Europe, which still endures and is underpinned by superpower competition. Very stimulating.

Deutsch, K. W., *et al.* (1969), *Political Community in the North Atlantic Area* (Westport, Conn.: Greenwood Press). Originally published in 1957 by Princeton University Press. A seminal attempt to analyse the North Atlantic area as a nascent 'community' bound together by transactions and the growth of responsiveness.

Diebold, W. (1959), *The Schuman Plan* (New York: Praeger). A very full treatment of the origins and implications of the European Coal and Steel Community, showing that American attitudes were not by any means wholeheartedly in favour of it on economic grounds (but also that 'political' motives were more important at the time).

Diebold, W. (1960), 'The changed economic position of Western Europe: some implications for US policy and international organization', *International Organization*, vol. 14, no. 1, pp. 1–19. A very helpful article which reveals the tensions set up by West European recovery and the difficult choices of priorities with which this confronted the Americans.

Diebold, W. (1980), *Industrial Policy as an International Issue* (New York: McGraw-Hill for Council on Foreign Relations). An important study of what in the 1980s was to become a major area of contention between the United States and Western Europe, both at the governmental and private levels.

Dönhoff, M. (1979), 'Bonn and Washington: the strained relationship', *Foreign Affairs*, vol. 57, no. 5, pp. 1052–64. One of a number of articles on this subject, published in the late 1970s and early 1980s, and focusing on the increasing divergence of American and West German views on security and economic policy.

Duroselle, J.-B. (1977), 'France and the West: concerns and fears', *Review of Politics*, vol. 39, no. 4, pp. 451–72. Demonstrates some important aspects of the 'Eurocommunism' phenomenon, which was shortlived but much-noticed while it lasted.

Earle, E. M. (1951), 'The American stake in Europe: retrospect and prospect', *International Affairs*, vol. 27, no. 4, pp. 423–33. Earle takes a historical as well as an analytical perspective to gauge the implications of the Americans' new involvements.

Eden, A. (1960), *Memoirs: Full Circle* (London: Cassell). Especially revealing on the British role in (and attitude towards) the European Defence Community, 'summitry' and NATO. The American role in the Suez crisis also looms large.

Eisenhower, D. (1963), *The White House Years. Vol. I, Mandate for Change,*

1953–1956 (London: Heinemann). Several chapters reveal the development of American views on NATO (and especially West Germany's role). It is an interesting contrast to Eden.

Eisenhower, D. (1966), *The White House Years. Vol. II, Waging Peace, 1956–1961* (London: Heinemann). Again, there is valuable material here on the problems of NATO strategy, proposals for 'disengagement' and the emergence of the EEC (but this does not feature prominently).

Etzold, T., and Gaddis, J. L. (eds)(1978), *Containment: Documents on American Foreign Policy and Strategy, 1945–1950* (New York: Columbia University Press). One of the best collections, which has a substantial section on the implementation of containment in Europe, 1948–50.

Fedder, E. (1973), *NATO: The Dynamics of Alliance in the Postwar World* (New York: Dodd, Mead). More than just a survey or a description; Fedder tests the Alliance against existing theories and concepts of alliance politics, and produces some very interesting insights. It is a bit dated, but the ideas still apply.

Fedder, E. (ed.)(1980), *Defense Politics of the Atlantic Alliance* (New York: Praeger). A wide-ranging collection of national studies, as well as more general treatments of issues.

Feld, W. (ed.)(1978), *Western Europe's Global Reach: Regional Cooperation and Worldwide Aspirations* (New York and Oxford: Pergamon). Some interesting contributions which draw attention especially to European–American competition, as well as to the 'rules' of transatlantic economic relations.

Fox, W., and Fox, A. B. (1967), *NATO and the Range of American Choice* (New York: Columbia University Press). An important study of the American 'image' of NATO, and the role it played in United States' policy during the 1950s and 1960s.

Fox, W., and Schilling W. (ed.)(1973), *European Security and the Atlantic System* (New York and London: Columbia University Press). Draws attention to national dilemmas arising out of the development of détente and United States–Soviet negotiations.

Freedman, L. (1981–2), 'NATO myths', *Foreign Policy*, no. 45, pp. 48–68. Freedman sets out to establish the core of the Alliance and to cut away some at least of the extraneous and problematical beliefs which have come to surround it.

Freedman, L. (1982), 'The Atlantic crisis', *International Affairs*, vol. 58, no. 3, pp. 395–412. Exposes the dimensions of the crisis, which are seen as rooted in views of the world in general as well as in specific areas of contention.

Furniss, E. (1953), 'French attitudes toward Western European unity', *International Organization*, vol. 7, no. 2, pp. 199–212.

Furniss, E. (1956), 'France, NATO, and European security', *International Organization*, vol. 10, no. 4, pp. 544–58.

Furniss, E. (1961), 'De Gaulle's France and NATO: an interpretation', *International Organization*, vol. 15, no. 3, pp. 349–65. This and the other Furniss articles (see above) are useful assessments of developing French attitudes, which show some of the continuity of policy as well as the impact of De Gaulle.

Fursdon, E. (1980), *The European Defence Community: A History* (London: Macmillan). Deals with the background, in a way which reveals the impact of broader changes on European–American disputes.

Garfinkle, A. (1981), 'America and Europe in the Middle East: a new coordination?', *Orbis*, vol. 25, no. 3, pp. 631–48. Stresses need for co-ordination of policies which are basically parallel, but also recognises that mutual suspicions stand in the way. It advocates American use of closer West European links to the Arabs and PLO in furtherance of peace efforts.

Garnett, J. (1968), 'The United States and Europe: defence, technology and the Western Alliance', *International Affairs*, vol. 44, no. 2, pp. 282–8. A commentary on the 'technology gap' and the specific manifestations of this in the defence field.

Gatzke, H. (1980), *Germany and the United States: A 'Special Relationship'?* (Cambridge, Mass.: Harvard University Press). Interesting, because it puts a historical gloss upon the postwar problems and places the position of West Germany in a longer perspective.

Glass, G. (1979), 'The United States and West Germany: cracks in the security foundation', *Orbis*, vol. 25, no. 3, pp. 631–48. Points to the undermining of shared attitudes about détente and the Alliance.

Goodman, E. (1975), *The Fate of the Atlantic Community* (New York: Praeger). Goodman examines both the philosophical and material underpinning of the 'community' and the contentious issues of the 1970s (which are global as well as 'Atlantic' in origin).

Gordon, L. (1956a), 'The Organization for European Economic Cooperation', *International Organization*, vol. 10, no. 1, pp. 1–11. A general survey of the OEEC's work, especially in the light of the beginnings of the EEC.

Gordon, L. (1956b), 'Economic aspects of coalition diplomacy: the NATO experience', *International Organization*, vol. 10, no. 4, pp. 529–43. This is a valuable early (and still suggestive) attempt to assess the 'burden-sharing' problem in the light of strategic change and West European recovery.

Griffith, W. E. (1982), 'Bonn and Washington: from deterioration to crisis?', *Orbis*, vol. 26, no. 1, pp. 117–34. Assesses the impact of divergent security perceptions, especially in the light of nuclear policy.

Grosser, A. (1980), *The Western Alliance: The United States and Western Europe since 1945* (London: Macmillan). A large-scale and authoritative treatment of the French and West German positions in particular, but generally a very rich and instructive source on domestic as well as international political change. It is especially revealing on Kennedy and De Gaulle.

Hahn, W., and Pfaltzgraff, R. (eds)(1979), *Atlantic Community in Crisis: A Redefinition of the Transatlantic Relationship* (New York and Oxford: Pergamon). The contributors doggedly pursue the idea of a 'community' and in doing so produce a lot of useful evidence, not all of which sustains the case. A particularly useful chapter is by Diane Pfaltzgraff on the idea of an 'Atlantic Community'.

Hanrieder, W. (ed.)(1974), *The United States and Western Europe: Political, Economic and Strategic Perspectives* (Cambridge, Mass.: Winthrop). A very solid collection, especially on the economic side (see in particular the chapter by B. Cohen on the collapse of the 'transatlantic bargain'). Most contributors attempt a sober analysis of the 'Nixon Shock' and 'Nixon Doctrine'.

Hanrieder, W. (ed.)(1982), *Economic Issues and the Atlantic Community* (New York: Praeger). A sophisticated and valuable collection which focuses on the 'political economy' of issues arising from the recession of the 1970s and early 1980s, and relates domestic to international policies.

Harrison, M. (1981), *The Reluctant Ally: France and European Security* (Baltimore, Md, and London: Johns Hopkins University Press). A magisterial book, providing both an account of the underlying continuities in French attitudes to 'Atlanticism' and an appreciation of alliance theories.

Harrison, R. (1974), *Europe in Question: Theories of Regional International Integration* (London: Allen & Unwin). Perhaps the most useful general survey: it has one chapter dealing explicitly with the American role as an external integrating force, and another dealing with external relations of the EEC.

Henderson, M. (1981), 'The OECD as an instrument of national policy', *International Journal*, vol. 36, no. 4, pp. 793–814. Concentrates in particular on American dominance as pursued through the OECD.

Hinshaw, R. (1964), *The European Community and American Trade: A Study in Atlantic Economics and Policy* (New York: Praeger for Council on Foreign Relations). Another of the *Atlantic Policy Studies*.

Hoag, M. (1958), 'NATO: deterrent or shield?', *Foreign Affairs*, vol. 36, no. 2, pp. 278–92. Raises many of the questions about NATO as a nuclear or conventional alliance which have since become familiar currency.

Hoffmann, S. (1964–5), 'The European process at Atlantic cross-purposes', *Journal of Common Market Studies*, vol. 3, no. 2, pp. 85–101. A telling commentary on the clash between 'Europeanism' and 'Atlanticism' in the light of Gaullism.

Hoffmann, S. (1968), *Gulliver's Troubles, or the Setting of American Foreign Policy* (New York: McGraw-Hill for Council on Foreign Relations). Points up the paradoxes created by American global entanglement, with substantial studies of the 'Atlantic puzzle'.

Hoffmann, S. (1978), *Primacy or World Order: American Foreign Policy since the Cold War* (New York: McGraw-Hill). Aptly illustrates the growing uncertainies attending the United States' role, and articulates a strong plea for responsible and accountable American leadership.

Hoffman, S. (1979). 'New variations on old themes', *International Security*, vol. 4, no. 1, pp. 88–107. Draws attention to the historical antecedents of the 'new' crisis in NATO during the late 1970s.

Hoffman, S. (1981). 'The Western Alliance: drift or harmony?' *International Security*, vol. 6, no. 2, pp. 105–25. An extension of his argument in *Primacy or World Order* for the re-establishment of purposeful co-ordination between the United States and its allies.

Holmes, J. (1968), 'Fearful symmetry: the dilemmas of consultation and coordination in the North Atlantic Treaty Organization', *International Organisation*, vol 22, no. 4, pp. 821–40. A solid account of the political arguments and procedural changes produced in the late 1960s.

Hunter, R. (1969), *Security in Europe* (London: Elek). Thematic treatment which stresses the continuity of problems and provides background to the détente negotiations.

Ireland, T. (1981), *Creating the Entangling Alliance: The Origins of the North Atlantic Treaty Organization* (Westport, Conn.: Greenwood Press; London: Aldwych Press). A stimulating treatment, stressing the lack of overt 'design' in American policy, and also highlighting domestic factors.

Joffe, J. (1981), 'European–American relations: the enduring crisis', *Foreign Affairs*, vol. 59, no. 4, pp. 835–51. Draws attention to the divergent views of détente and its future in the wake of the Afghanistan crisis, and sees fundamental European–American tensions emerging.

Joffe, J. (1983), 'Europe and America: the politics of resentment (cont'd)', *Foreign Affairs*, vol. 61, no. 3, *America and the World* 1982, pp. 569–90. Draws attention to the dangers posed by a combination of European (especially West German) neutralism and American unilateralism and calls for renewed moderation and responsiveness.

Johnson, P. (1979), 'Washington and Bonn: dimensions of change in bilateral relations', *International Organization*, vol. 33, no. 4, pp. 451–80. Interesting attempt to apply an analytical framework to the system of relations between the United States and West Germany.

Kaiser, K. (1966–7), 'The United States and the EEC in the Atlantic system: the problem of theory', *Journal of Common Market Studies*, vol. 5, no. 3, pp. 388–425. Argues that the structure and functioning of the 'system' itself can be a cause for contention and conflict. It is an interesting attempt to think from first principles.

Kaiser, K. (1973), *Europe and America: The Future of the Relationship* (Washington, DC.: Columbia Books). A brief attempt at 'scenario-building', which produces some interesting possibilities but is handicapped by a rather sketchy analysis of background.

Kaiser, K. (1974), 'Europe and America: a critical phase', *Foreign Affairs*, vol. 52, no. 4, pp. 725–41. One of the most useful assessments of the 1973–4 crisis.

Kaiser, K. (1978) 'The great nuclear debate: German–American disagreements', *Foreign Policy*, no. 30, pp. 85–110. Contains much useful material on the Carter administration's policy in general as well as on specifically German responses.

Kaiser, K., and Schwartz, H-P. (eds)(1977), *America and Western Europe: Problems and Prospects* (Lexington, Mass.: D. C. Heath). Many of the most useful contributions here focus on cultural and elite underpinnings of Atlantic relations (and on their erosion).

Kaldor, M. (1979), *The Disintegrating West* (Harmondsworth: Penguin). A challenging, radical view of 'West–West' conflicts and their extension to the wider world; more readable than some analyses of American hegemony.

Kaufmann, W. (1964), *The McNamara Strategy* (New York: Harper & Row). Especially interesting on the 'selling' of 'flexible response' to the European allies.

Kelleher, K. M. (1975), *Germany and the Politics of Nuclear Weapons* (New York and London: Columbia University Press). A well-documented and substantial account of the issues raised, both within and outside West Germany.

Keohane, R., and Nye, J. (1977), *Power and Interdependence: World Politics in Transition* (Boston, Mass.: Little, Brown). Juxtaposes interpretations based on 'realism' and 'complex interdependence'. The early chapters are especially lucid and relevant.

King, K. (1982), *US Monetary Policy and European Responses in the 1980s* (London: Routledge & Kegan Paul for Royal Institue of International Affairs). One of the *Chatham House Papers*; a brief account which is most illuminating on the changes in priorities and available techniques for constructing macroeconomic policy.

Kissinger, H. (1957), *Nuclear Weapons and Foreign Policy* (New York: Harper). Focuses above all on the increased delicacy of alliance politics in the nuclear age, and the implications for American policy in NATO. A very important source.

Kissinger, H. (1960), *The Necessity for Choice: Prospects of American Foreign Policy* (New York: Harper & Row). Carries further the argument in *Nuclear Weapons and Foreign Policy*; the case is made for responsible leadership, but also for some devolution of power to allies.

Kissinger, H. (1965), *The Troubled Partnership: A Reappraisal of the Atlantic Alliance* (New York: McGraw-Hill for Council on Foreign Relations). Kissinger's contribution to the Atlantic Policy Studies series. Again, it argues the case for allies to be given a more responsible role.

Kissinger, H. (1979), *The White House Years* (London: Weidenfeld & Nicolson/Michael Joseph). Memoirs of the first Nixon administration, with much useful material on Atlantic relations (although other issues significantly take up more of the author's attention).

Kissinger, H. (1982), *Years of Upheaval* (London: Weidenfeld & Nicolson/Michael Joseph). As for *The White House Years* – but contains Kissinger's reflections on the 'Year of Europe' and the 1973–4 crises.

Kleiman, R. (1964), *Atlantic Crisis: American Diplomacy Confronts a Resurgent Europe* (New York: W. W. Norton). One of the cluster of books which drew attention to the tensions caused by Kennedy's 'grand design' and its confrontation with both Gaullism and the EEC.

Knorr, K. (ed.) (1959), *NATO and American Security* (Princeton, NJ: Princeton University Press). Contains some important reflections on the changes of the late 1950s and the new pressures these imposed on the Alliance.

Kohl, W. (1971), *French Nuclear Diplomacy* (Princeton, NJ: Princeton University Press). A clear account of the antecedents as well as the De Gaulle years.

Kohl, W. (1975), 'The Nixon–Kissinger foreign policy system and US–European relations: patterns of policy making', *World Politics*, vol. 28, no. 1, pp. 1–43. A most interesting analysis which proceeds from the assumption that the ways in which American policy was made had an important bearing on the Atlantic conflicts of the Nixon years.

Kolko, J., and Kolko, G. (1972), *The Limits of Power: The World and US Foreign Policy, 1945–1954* (New York: Harper & Row). A very detailed 'revisionist' study, arguing that American policy set out to form the world after a pattern desired by economic and military interests. There are several interesting chapters on the Marshall Plan and Nato.

Kolodziej, E. (1980–1), 'Europe: the partial partner', *International Security*, vol. 5, no. 3, pp. 104–31. Strongly critical of the West Europeans' desire to retain American protection while being unable (or unwilling) to contribute more in the military field and competing strongly in the economic arena.

Kraft, J. (1962), *The Grand Design: From Common Market to Atlantic Partnership* (New York: Harper). Makes it very apparent that the 'grand design' was seen as a way of controlling the EEC as well as acknowledging its increased status. Kraft was a journalist close to the Kennedy administration.

Krause, L. (1968), *European Economic Integration and the United States* (Washington, DC: Brookings Institution). Perhaps the best economic interpretation of the EEC's impact. It is sometimes a bit technical, but the argument is generally very clear and points to the gains (for the United States) outweighing the losses.

Krause, L. (1969), 'The impact of economic relations on the Atlantic Alliance', *Orbis*, vol. 13, no. 1, pp. 270–86. Another of the relatively few treatments of this important underlying issue.

Krause, L., and Salant, W. (eds) (1973), *European Monetary Integration and its Meaning for the United States* (Washington, DC: Brookings Institution). This is a major collection of papers surveying the implications of what seemed at the time to be a new stage in European integration; a very useful indication of American attitudes more generally.

Landes, D. (ed.) (1977), *Western Europe: The Trials of Partnership* (Lexington, Mass.: D. C. Heath). One of a series of collections entitled 'Critical choices for Americans', but despite the title a very solid collection. Not surprisingly, given the date of publication, Eurocommunism looms large.

Lawson, R. (1958), 'Concerting policies in the North Atlantic Community', *International Organization*, vol. 12, no. 2, pp. 163–179. Useful for the view it gives of the 'political consultation' machinery.

Layton, C. (1968), *Transatlantic Investments* (Boulogne-sur-Seine: The Atlantic Institute). A comprehensive study, with much useful data, of the extent to which and the ways in which American firms had 'invaded' Western Europe during the 1960s.

Lerner, D., and Aron, R. (eds) (1957), *France Defeats EDC* (New York: Praeger). A series of essays analysing the internal and external ramifications of the French crisis over the European Defence Community. It is valuable for its linking of internal French politics with the Atlantic dimension.

Lieber, R. (1974), 'Europe and America in the world energy crisis', *International Affairs*, vol. 55, no. 4, pp. 552–7. One of a number of contributions made by Lieber on this subject, and dealing with the problems of co-ordinating Atlantic policies.

Lieber, R. (1980), 'Economics, energy, and security in Alliance perspective', *International Security*, vol. 4, no. 4, pp. 139–63. Especially useful in the light of events under the Carter administration and the second oil crisis of 1979–80.

Lunn, S. (1983), *Burden Sharing in NATO* (London: Routledge & Kegan Paul for Royal Institute of International Affairs). One of the *Chatham House Papers*, giving a valuable up-to-date view of a longstanding Alliance problem.

McGeehan, R. (1971), *The German Rearmament Question: American Diplomacy and European Defense after World War II* (Urbana, Ill.: University of Illinois Press). Most comprehensive treatment of this contentious issue of the 1940s and 1950s; an extensive historical study.

McNamara, R. (1968), *The Essence of Security: Reflections in Office* (London: Hodder & Stoughton). Interesting memoir by the originator of the McNamara Doctrine, which has much to say about the rationale for 'flexible response'.

Mally, G. (ed.) (1974), *The New Europe and the United States: Partners or Rivals?* (Lexington, Mass.: D. C. Heath for Atlantic Council of the United States). Wide-ranging collection of academic asessments and policy-makers' statements, giving a good indication of the flavour of debate in the early 1970s.

Malmgren, H. (1970–1), 'Coming trade wars?', *Foreign Policy*, no. 1, pp. 115–43. Sets out the evidence for a politicisation of trade policy, and reviews the dangers of conflicts between the United States and Western Europe (among others).

Mandel, E. (1970), *Europe versus America? Contradictions of Imperialism* (London: New Left Books). Argues that American capitalism and its expansion into Europe has called forth a rival (the EEC) which will come to form a second major concentration of capital. It is one of the central statements from this school of thought.

Mandelbaum, M. (1979), *The Nuclear Question: The United States and Nuclear Weapons, 1946–1976* (Cambridge: Cambridge University Press). Important historical survey which points out the continuity of the problem.

Manderson-Jones, R. (1972), *The Special Relationship: Anglo-American Relations and West European Unity, 1947–1956* (London: Weidenfeld & Nicolson). An assessment of British policy in particular, which points out the fact that British leaders' views of their role *vis-à-vis* Europe were fundamentally at odds with those of most American policy-makers.

Miller, L. (1974), *The Limits of Alliance: America, Europe, and the Middle East* (Jerusalem: Hebrew University Press for Leonard Davis Institute for International Relations). A brief but very useful review both of the continuing tensions and the particular problems which erupted in 1973–4.

Monnet, J. (1978), *Memoirs* (London: Collins). Monnet was one of the chief architects of European integration, but saw it firmly within an Atlantic framework. The memoirs are a vital source for understanding of the postwar 'Atlantic elite'. (See also Ball, 1982.)

Morgan, R. (1974), *The United States and West Germany, 1945–1973: A Study in Alliance Politics* (London: Oxford University Press for Royal Institute of International Affairs). Morgan sets up a framework for analysis for this relationship stressing the importance of domestic, regional and 'Atlantic' elements. While sometimes a bit cumbersome, it is a valuable source of questions about the complexity of European–American relations in general, as well as German–American links.

Munk, F. (1964), *Atlantic Dilemma: Partnership or Community?* (Dobbs Ferry, NY: Oceana). One of the spate of books which resulted from Kennedy's 'grand design' and the growing awareness of European assertiveness; has the merit of stating the central issues clearly and dispassionately.

Nau, H. (1971), 'A political interpretation of the technology gap dispute', *Orbis*, vol. 15, no. 2, pp. 507–27. Interesting assessment of one of the major dimensions in the 'American challenge' of the late 1960s.

Neustadt, R. (1970), *Alliance Politics* (New York: Columbia University Press). A study of the British–American relationship in the 1950s and 1960s, stressing the intimacy of the links between the governments concerned. It reveals that the assumed convergence of policies can lead to misperceptions and the exacerbation of differences.

Newhouse, J., Croan, M., *et al.* (1971), *United States Troops in Europe: Issues, Costs, and Choices* (Washington, DC: Brookings Institution). Covers the debates which centred around the question of 'offset payments' and congressional calls for troop withdrawals.

Nicholas, H. G. (1978), *The United States and Great Britain* (Chicago: Chicago University Press). A broad historical survey; the last four chapters are useful for the post-1945 period.

Orbis (1973), 'The Year of Europe', *Orbis*, vol. 17, no. 1. This is a special issue of the journal with a number of articles focused on the Kissinger initiative (before the rot set in later in the year).

Orbis (1980), 'The Atlantic nations in the 1978–79 oil crisis', *Orbis*, vol. 23, no. 4. Another special issue, this one concentrating on the transatlantic discord caused by the dislocations of the second oil 'shock'.

Osgood, R. (1962), *NATO: The Entangling Alliance* (Chicago: Chicago University Press). A classic study of NATO, which focuses especially on the politics of American involvement and the development of 'alliance politics'. Indispensable both for its analysis and its place in debates about Atlantic strategy.

Osgood, R. (1968), *Alliances and American Foreign Policy* (Baltimore, Md, and London: Johns Hopkins University Press). The section on 'Alliances in Europe' is good as a general review, but the value of this book also lies in its overall treatment of the Americans' alliance policies.

Osgood, R. *et al.* (1973), *Retreat from Empire? The First Nixon Administration* (Baltimore, Md, and London: Johns Hopkins University Press). A series of substantial essays covering the new direction given to American foreign policy by the Nixon–Kissinger approach. Especially useful chapters are by Osgood and Calleo.

Oye, K., Rothschild, R., and Lieber, R. (eds) (1979), *Eagle Entangled: US Foreign Policy in a Complex World* (New York and London: Longman). Reflects the new-found complexity of the Carter administration's world. Some very interesting contributions are on industrial and energy policy, as well as the public mood in the United States itself.

Padelford, N. (1955), 'Political cooperation in the North Atlantic Community', *International Organization*, vol. 9, no. 3, pp. 353–65. An early contribution to the literature on NATO as a political rather than simply a military entity.

Patterson, G., and Furniss, E. (eds) (1957), *NATO: A Critical Appraisal* (Princeton. NJ: Princeton University Press). An important set of articles reviewing the tensions and contradictions which had emerged within the Alliance by the late 1950s.

Pfaltzgraff, R. (1969), *The Atlantic Community: A Complex Imbalance* (New York: Van Nostrand Reinhold). A fairly short but stimulating survey of the various issue-areas around which debate centred in the late 1960s; especially strong on the breakdown of consensus at the strategic level.

Pfaltzgraff, R. (1975), 'The American–European–Japanese relationship: prospects for the late 1970s', *Orbis*, vol. 19, no. 3, pp. 809–26. During the late 1970s the idea of 'trilateralism' – a kind of partnership including Japan as well as the United States and Western Europe – had considerable currency. This article expresses some of the hopes and concerns, although later events especially in the economic field eroded the hopes somewhat.

Pierre, A. J. (1973), 'Can Europe's security be 'decoupled' from America?' *Foreign Affairs*, vol. 51, no. 4, pp. 761–77. A much-reprinted article exposing in a clear form the potential for 'disengagement' which worried so many in the early 1980s.

Platt, A., and Leonardi, R. (1978), 'American foreign policy and the postwar Italian Left', *Political Science Quarterly*, vol. 93, no. 2, pp. 197–215. Very interesting review of American attitudes and interventions, giving good background to fears of Eurocommunism.

Preeg, E. (1970), *Traders and Diplomats: An analysis of the Kennedy Round of Negotiations under the General Agreement on Tariffs and Trade* (Washington DC: Brookings Institution). Very full account by an experienced official, revealing the awkwardness caused by the multilevel nature of policy-making in the EEC, with valuable detail on the agreements reached.

Ranger, R. (1981), 'NATO's new great debate: theatre nuclear force modernization and arms control', *International Journal*, vol. 36, no. 3, pp. 556–74. Sets out clearly the issues which created differences and suspicions during the early parts of the Reagan presidency.

Richardson, J. (1964–5), 'The concept of the Atlantic Community', *Journal of Common Market Studies*, vol. 3, no. 1, pp. 1–22. One of the best discussions of the problem in its theoretical dimesion, revealing divergent perceptions of the concept.

Richardson, J. (1966). *Germany and the Atlantic Alliance: The Interaction of Strategy and Politics* (Cambridge, Mass.: Harvard University Press). A major study which is especially strong on the domestic political implications of integration into NATO.

Rosecrance, R. (ed.) (1976), *America as an Ordinary Country: US Foreign Policy and the Future* (Ithaca, NY: Cornell University Press). Series of papers taking as their starting-point the perceived change in American status since 1970. Many reveal the rather contradictory implication of 'ordinariness' for the world's largest economic and military power, and several focus on the implications for Western Europe.

Schaetzel, J. (1975), *The Unhinged Alliance: America and the European Community* (New York: Harper & Row for Council on Foreign Relations). The author was head of the US Mission to the EEC, and has a generally critical view of the way in which successive United States administrations neglected the problem of European integration. He is especially severe on the Nixon–Kissinger approach.

Scheingold, S. (1971), 'The North Atlantic area as a policy arena'. *International Studies Quarterly*, vol. 15, no. 1, pp. 32–65. A most useful article. Scheingold surveys existing attempts to conceptualise the North Atlantic area, and goes on to develop the idea of the 'policy arena' which poses problems for the formulation and pursuit of policy objectives.

Schilling, W., *et al.* (1973), *American Arms and a Changing Europe: Dilemmas of Deterrence and Disarmament* (New York: Columbia University Press). Especially illuminating on the problem of troop reductions, also on the impact of détente on European countries in general and particular cases.

Schlesinger, A. M. (ed.)(1973), *Dynamics of World Power: A Documentary History of American Foreign Policy, 1945–1973. Vol. 2, Western Europe* (New York: McGraw-Hill). A massive collection, essential to detailed study and covering all major areas of policy.

Serfaty, S. (1979), *Fading Partnership: America and Europe after Thirty Years* (New York: Praeger). Adopts the line that a combination of American policies and developments in West European countries have eroded the basis of alliance. It is strong on domestic developments, with a good treatment of American attitudes towards the Left in Europe.

Scrvan-Schreiber, J.-J. (1968), *The American Challenge* (London: Hamish Hamilton). Seminal contribution to the controversy over American multinationals, the 'technology gap' and the call for a concerted European response (although much of the argument is also distinctively French in character).

Shonfield, A., *et al.* (1976), *International Economic Relations of the Western World, 1959–1971*, 2 vols (London: Oxford University Press for Royal Institute of International Affairs). Large-scale survey of trade (Vol. 1) and monetary (Vol. 2) relations in what might be seen as the heyday of the Bretton Woods system. Shonfield's 'overview' chapter in Vol 1 is an especially valuable survey, detailing the erosion of American hegemony and the breakdown of Bretton Woods.

Smith, M. (1978), 'From the "Year of Europe" to a year of Carter: continuing patterns and problems in Euro-American relations', *Journal of Common Market Studies*, vol. 17, no. 1, pp. 26–44. Reviews the debates of the mid-1970s and puts forward a number of systemic and policy-making factors which might account for continued suspicions and tensions.

Smith, M. (1981), 'Britain and the United States in the Eighties: fragmentation and the policy agenda'. *Yearbook of World Affairs*, pp. 165–80. Explores the changing substance of British–American relations and the impact on them of trends in domestic and international contexts.

Smith, M., Little, R., and Shackleton, M. (eds)(1981), *Perspectives on World Politics* (London: Croom Helm). Contains edited selections which contrast approaches to world politics based on 'power and security', 'interdependence' and 'dominance and dependence', as well as some which apply these views.

Sommer, T. (1980), 'Europe and the American connection', *Foreign Affairs*, vol. 58, no. 3, *America and the World 1979*, pp. 622–36. Assesses the impact of strategic and economic factors in a year of considerable upheaval.

Spero, J. (1981), *The Politics of International Economic Relations*, 2nd edn (London: Allen & Unwin). Pt II is a very useful survey of the 'Western system' which exposes the assumptions and procedures behind commercial and financial dealings.

Spiegel, S. (ed.) (1982), *The Middle East and the Western Alliance* (London: Allen & Unwin). Strong collection which points to the continuing problems posed by 'out of area' conflicts, and to the impact of European Political Co-operation.

Stanley, T. (1965), *Nato in Transition: The Future of the Atlantic Alliance* (New York: Praeger for Council on Foreign Relations). Adopts both a historical approach and an analytical method aimed at assessing major issues and their possible future development. Draws attention to the 'political economy' of NATO in the mid-1960s.

Storey, J. (1981), 'The Federal Republic: a conservative revisionist', *West European Politics*, vol. 4, no. 2, pp. 56–86. Very informative article, especially where it links domestic economic and political priorities to international connections in Europe and with the United States.

Treverton, G. (1979), 'Nuclear weapons and the "grey area" ', *Foreign Affairs*, vol. 57, no. 5, pp. 1975–89. Emphasises some of the central problems attending arms control efforts in the late 1970s, particularly the difficulty of defining new types of weapon.

Treverton, G. (1980), 'Global threats and trans-Atlantic allies', *International Security*, vol. 5, no. 2, pp. 142–58. Draws attention to the divergent perceptions of threat held in the United States under Reagan and in Western Europe (particularly West Germany).

Trezise, P. (1975), *The Atlantic Connection: Prospects, Problems and Policies* (Washington, DC: Brookings Institution). A neat, brief setting-out of the policy agenda as seen by an acute observer; covers economic, strategic and broader political issues, stressing common interests as well as differences.

Trezise, P. (ed.)(1979), *The European Monetary System: Its Promise and Prospects* (Washington, DC: Brookings Institution). Useful collection of papers illustrating technical and political aspects of the EMS, and implications for the United States.

Triffin, R. (1978–9), 'The international role and fate of the dollar', *Foreign Affairs*, vol. 57, no. 2, pp. 269–86. A view of the situation in the late 1970s – a time of dollar weakness – by one of the longstanding experts on the Atlantic monetary system.

Truman, H. (1965), *Memoirs. Vol. II, Years of Trial and Hope, 1946–1952 (New*

York: Signet). Valuable material on the Marshall Plan, NATO and the crises of the late 1940s and early 1950s; an important source.

Tucker, R. (1981), *The Purposes of American Power: An Essay on National Security* (New York: Praeger). Tucker proposes a foreign policy of 'moderate realism' to replace the global ambitions of earlier periods (and the drift of the Carter period, on which he is severe).

Tucker, R., and Wrigley, L. (eds) (1983), *The Atlantic Alliance and its Critics* (New York: Praeger). A collection of reflective pieces which put the strategic and accompanying political problems of the 1980s into a valuable broader perspective.

Vandenburg, A. (ed.) (1953), *The Private Papers of Senator Vandenburg* (London: Gollancz). Revealing diary-cum-memoirs of one of the chief actors in the dramas of the late 1940s. Vandenburg was fearful of 'neo-isolationism' and played a major role in asserting the need for American involvement in Europe.

Vannicelli, P. (1974), *Italy, NATO and the European Community: The Interplay of Foreign Policy and Domestic Politics*, Harvard Studies in International Affairs, No. 31 (Harvard, Mass.: Center for International Affairs). A brief (but almost the only) study, which makes some very interesting points about the 'Atlantic' or 'European' priorities of Italian political groupings, over the postwar period in general.

Vernon, R. (1971), *Sovereignty at Bay: The Multinational Spread of US Enterprises* (London: Longman). One of the major early studies of the problem, which has much material on the *modus operandi* of the multinationals in the North Atlantic area.

Vernon, R. (1973), 'Rogue elephant in the forest: an appraisal of transatlantic relations', *Foreign Affairs*, vol. 51, no. 3, pp. 573–87. Centres on the disruptions caused by the American pursuit of national interests at the expense of consultation and co-ordination.

Vernon, R. (ed.)(1976), *The Oil Crisis* (New York: W. W. Norton). Major collection of papers documenting American reactions in particular, and revealing European–American divergence at many points.

Wallace, W. (1976), 'Issue linkage among Atlantic governments', *International Affairs*, vol. 52, no. 2, pp. 163–79. Interesting attempt to identify both the use of 'linkage' as a foreign policy weapon, forcing trade-offs and compromises, and the impact of unmanaged linkages between societies in conditions of interdependence.

Wallerstein, I. (1980), 'Friends as foes', *Foreign Policy*, no. 40, pp. 119–31. Clear statement of the argument that structural conflict between Western Europe and the United States is unavoidable given the development of their economic and political systems; implies that there may be radical realignments in the future.

Wallich, H. (1968), 'The US and the EEC: a problem of adjustment', *International Organization*, vol. 22, no. 4, pp. 841–54. An economist's view which stresses the technical impact of shifts in the economic 'balance of power' – useful because of this approach, but leaves a lot of 'political' questions to be answered.

Walton, A.-M. (1976), 'Atlantic bargaining over energy', *International Affairs*, vol. 52, no. 2, pp. 180–96. Follows the framework set out in Wallace (1976) and demonstrates the complexity of interests and institutions confronted with the 1973–4 oil crisis.

Warnecke, S. (ed.) (1972), *The European Community in the 1970s* (New York: Praeger). General collection of pieces on the EEC, with several interesting chapters dealing with Atlantic trade and financial relations.

Webb, C. (1979), *Eurocommunism and Foreign Policy* (London: Policy Studies Institute). Perhaps the best and most dispassionate assessment of the extent to which Eurocommunism threatened a real change in foreign policy orientations within Western Europe.

Whitman, M. (1975), 'Leadership without hegemony', *Foreign Policy*, no. 20, pp. 138–61. Stimulating assessment of the erosion of American dominance which also points to the continuing need for leadership and responsible action.

Wilcox, F., and Haviland, H. F. (eds)(1963), *The Atlantic Community: Progress and Prospects* (New York: Praeger). Major collection containing many important assessments. It can also be found as a special issue of *International Organization*, and has the great merit of gathering together analytical pieces and contributions from policy-makers.

Williams, G. (1977), *The Permanent Alliance: The European–American Partnership, 1945–1984* (Leyden: Sijthoff). A compendious but slightly uneven review of the strategic links in particular; lots of information, sometimes a bit difficult to get at. The predictions for 1984 make interesting reading!

Williams, P. (1982), 'Europe, America and the Soviet threat', *World Today*, vol. 38, no. 10, pp. 372–81. A penetrating analysis, which has the merit of comparing past problems with troop withdrawals and the American 'presence' with the situation in the 1980s, and comes to what may appear ominous conclusions.

Willis, F. R. (1968), *France, Germany and the New Europe, 1945–1967*, 2nd edn (London: Oxford University Press). Very thorough and well-argued treatment of the central thread in European integration, important to an understanding of the reception accorded American plans in the 1960s.

Willis, F. R. (1971), *Italy Chooses Europe* (New York: Oxford University Press). Does something of the same job for Italy as the preceding treatment of France and Germany; and draws attention to the important American role in anchoring Italy to the Western Alliance.

Wohlstetter, A. (1961), 'Nuclear sharing – NATO and the N + 1 country', *Foreign Affairs*, vol. 39, no. 3, pp. 355–87. Important article by a very well-informed strategist, raising many of the problems relating to nuclear control and proliferation.

Wolfers, A. (1958), 'Europe and the NATO shield', *International Organization* vol. 12, no. 4, pp. 425–39. Contribution to the debate over the role of nuclear and conventional forces in Western Europe, which was given added point by the emergence of tactical nuclear weapons in the late 1950s.

Wolfers, A. (ed.) (1964), *Changing East–West Relations and the Unity of the West* (Baltimore, Md: Johns Hopkins University Press). A bit ahead of its time, since it presages many of the issues which were to be raised in acute form by détente in the late 1960s

Woolcock, S. (1982), *Western Policies on East–West Trade* (London: Routledge & Kegan Paul for Royal Institute of International Affairs). Short but very solid and well-informed review of the history and recent content of disputes over 'trading with the enemy'. It points to differences of interpretation and needs between the United States and several West European countries.

Zahnser, M. (1975), *Uncertain Friendship: American–French Diplomatic Relations through the Cold War* (New York and London: Wiley). Provides a neat and comprehensive view of this rather troubled 'special relationship'.

Zoppo, C. E. (1980), 'The Left and European security: France, Italy, and Spain', *Orbis*, vol, 24, no. 2, pp. 289–310. Extends the evaluation of Eurocomunism and Eurosocialism beyond the high point of mid-1970s fears.

Index